COOK COLOUR

COOK
COLOUR

A RAINBOW OF 100 RECIPES

/

MARIA ZIZKA
photographs by David Malosh

Artisan | New York

ALSO BY MARIA ZIZKA

The Newlywed Table

One-Bowl Meals

Boards, Platters, Plates

Copyright © 2023 by Maria Zizka
Photographs copyright © 2023 by David Malosh

Library of Congress Cataloging-in-Publication Data is on file.
ISBN 9781648293245

Design by Vanessa Holden

Artisan books are available at special discounts when purchased in
bulk for premiums and sales promotions as well as for fundraising or
educational use. Special editions or book excerpts can also be created to
specification. For details, please contact special.markets@hbgusa.com.

The publisher is not responsible for websites (or their content) that are
not owned by the publisher.

The Hachette Speakers Bureau provides a wide range of authors for
speaking events. To find out more, go to hachettespeakersbureau.com or
email HachetteSpeakers@hbgusa.com.

Published by Artisan, an imprint of Workman Publishing Co., Inc.,
a subsidiary of Hachette Book Group, Inc.
1290 Avenue of the Americas
New York, NY 10104
artisanbooks.com

Artisan is a registered trademark of Workman Publishing Co., Inc.,
a subsidiary of Hachette Book Group, Inc.

Printed in China on responsibly sourced paper

First printing, April 2023

10 9 8 7 6 5 4 3 2 1

For **JOY** that follows sorrow,

For **RAINBOW BABIES** everywhere,

A LOVE LETTER to my Arthur

CONTENTS

/

WHAT DOES IT MEAN TO COOK BY COLOR?

When you gradually add cream to an iced coffee, as you stir and watch for the drink to turn teddy-bear brown, you are cooking by color. When you bake chocolate chip cookies and you wait until they are the perfect golden shade before you pull them out of the oven, you are cooking by color. When you combine ripe red cherries, raspberries, and plums to make a monochromatic salad, you are cooking by color.

Cooking by color is a joyful approach that feels celebratory but also experimental and even sometimes avant-garde. Flavor and color are often intertwined, and there's a satisfaction to cooking and eating something that tastes just like it looks. Our eyes see a certain color, our brain imagines specific textures and flavors, and our tongue confirms those expectations. In the same way that solving a puzzle feels rewarding, so, too, does using all our senses to create beautiful and delicious food.

This book will show you how to make food that radiates a particular hue in all its glory. Cooking this way will awaken your visual sense, teach you new techniques in the kitchen, and elevate your party-planning skills. As you cook your way through these recipes, you will begin to see raw ingredients in an entirely new light, and you'll become more excited about your own ability to boldly embrace all the colorful foods—from white to black and every hue in between.

The recipes are organized as a gradient, beginning with white recipes, moving on to yellow, orange, and red, followed by pink, purple, blue, green, and brown, and concluding with the grand finale of black recipes. Every section contains dishes that draw inspiration from across the globe, crossing borders and combining ingredients from different cultures. Color is the driving force that unifies them all. These recipes are not traditional. They are playful and creative. They are not afraid to break rules.

After you've cooked in color a few times, you'll be ready to start combining recipes to put together a color menu. Whether you're planning a holiday feast or celebrating your favorite team's championship win, check out Color Menus on page 228 for guidance and inspiration.

A NOTE ON INGREDIENTS

The recipes in *Cook Color* don't use artificial food coloring. There's no need when beets are already a rich magenta and purple potatoes look like the starry midnight sky. Some of the ingredients called for in these recipes are super specific. To achieve the intended color, you should avoid substitutions and seek out good-quality ingredients (see Sources, page 238). Even so, no two tomatoes will look exactly alike, and despite your best efforts, the dish you cook may appear to be a slightly different shade than the one in the photograph. That is okay! In fact, it's a beautiful thing that your color cooking will be influenced by where you live and where your food is grown.

1 SEASONALITY

Imagine strolling through a farmers market in October. What colors do you see? Pops of bright orange; shades of beige, tan, and brown; the forest green of lacinato kale, perhaps? You can guess the time of year simply by looking at the fruits and vegetables currently in season. Each season has its own spectacular color palette. When you are cooking by color, you'll achieve the best colors by using ingredients that are at their peak. An ear of yellow corn that's fresh from the field will be the most vibrant and will taste the most delicious. Also, fresh local produce tends to be more affordable than produce grown far away and transported to where you are. The recipes in this book celebrate the natural beauty of colorful foods and try to honor them by bringing out their hues. As a wonderful bonus, eating all the colors of the rainbow is one of the easiest and most delicious ways to eat nutritiously. The pigments that make foods colorful are important for our bodies to function and heal. Red and purple foods, rich in anthocyanins, may help prevent cardiovascular disease. Curcuminoids, the yellow pigments responsible for turmeric's golden hue, have powerful anti-inflammatory properties. Often, the bolder the color, the greater the health boost and the more intense the flavor will be. Color, health, and flavor go hand in hand.

2

TECHNIQUE

When you focus primarily on the color of ingredients, you'll see how they change when heated, chilled, cut, or exposed to acids like lemon juice. You'll find that the colors of some ingredients are especially sensitive to certain cooking techniques (like broiling or blanching, for example) and to the chemical makeup of foods they are paired with. The more you cook with attention to color, the more you'll pick up on the techniques best suited for achieving your desired results.

HEAT
BOILING

/

Raw asparagus spears are grass green. When boiled, their color slowly transforms to a more saturated green. You know the asparagus has cooked long enough to be tender when it turns a very specific shade—like a midwestern summer lawn after a rainstorm. If you cook asparagus too long, that green hue becomes muddy, dull, and brown. Remove the spears from the hot water as soon as they're done and drop them into an ice-water bath to stop the cooking process and capture that gorgeous color.

HEAT
CARAMELIZATION

/

Sliced white and yellow onions are close to pure white. If you cook them in a skillet, they turn golden. And if you keep cooking them, they caramelize to a deep amber shade.

17

NATURAL DYE
RED CABBAGE

/

Raw red cabbage is purple-red. It retains this color even after being simmered in a pot of water for 30 minutes or more. You can add a splash of white vinegar to set the color and use it as a natural dye for other ingredients, such as eggs. If you place boiled eggs in the cabbage liquid, their white shells will become dyed—but maybe not the color you're expecting. After about an hour, the eggshells will be pale blue. Eight hours later, they'll be indigo.

NATURAL DYE
BUTTERFLY PEA FLOWERS

/

Dried butterfly pea flowers have dusty, sun-faded blue blossoms. As soon as you pour boiling water over them to steep them into a tea, they turn bright royal blue, and the color intensifies with time. Add a squeeze of fresh lemon juice and—surprise! The blue shifts to purple.

WATER-SOLUBLE ANTHO-CYANINS

BLUEBERRIES

/

Fresh whole blueberries are the color of the cold depths of the Atlantic Ocean. Sliced in half, they are green inside! Cooked with sugar and lemon juice in a saucepan until jammy, their color transforms once again to purple.

3

PLATING

The way you compose a dish matters—and greatly affects its color. A white plate is a solid, neutral starting point. White looks like a matte border around a piece of art in a frame. Its blankness helps to center and highlight the color of the food you've cooked. But you can also try using plates and bowls that are the same color as the food to see how that changes the dish's appearance. You might consider trying a plate that is a contrasting color. Have fun with this final step of the cooking process, and toss out any ideas you have about the "right" way to put food on a plate. The recipes in this book offer plating suggestions, but feel free to experiment with layering the components of a dish. You may find new ways to showcase a dish's color. For example, a sauce can be spread across a plate or drizzled on top of the food. Think of yourself as an expert food stylist, and remember that your primary goal is to highlight the beautiful color you've cooked.

COLOR
BY COLOR

WHITE
/

White is the color of the heavens. Michelangelo chose white marble as his medium for sculpting *David*. A bride wears white on her wedding day. But white also symbolizes death, and in India, mourners wear white. White foods may seem like a blank canvas. However, if you look closely, you will see that there is always a little bit of color in any white food. A daikon radish is white, with just a hint of green around the top, which makes sense given that it grew on a leafy green plant. Daikon grows mostly underground, just as carrots do, with the shoulders of the vegetable poking up out of the dirt. The part that remains buried is not exposed to sunlight and stays white. Similarly, white asparagus is grown entirely underground (or, less bucolically, sometimes tarped with plastic). This keeps the spears milky white because without exposure to sunlight, no photosynthesis can occur. White rice is not purely white, either. All white rice starts as brown rice, with a husk, bran, and germ in place. During the milling process, the brown parts are removed. White rice retains a very slight tint of brown, like a shadow of its former self. As soon as you begin cooking with white ingredients and applying heat to them, you'll see that their color tends to shift, most often from white to brown. That is why many of the recipes in the white section of the book employ cooking methods that use indirect heat like poaching, boiling, and steeping. These gentle processes help to preserve the snowy colors. Toward the end of the white section, the dishes begin to move in the direction of yellow. Chicken Congee (page 38) is white but shimmers with a subtle golden hue from the

chicken fat. Garlicky Gigante Beans, Salt-and-Vin Cauliflower, and Pine Nuts (page 46) gets even closer to yellow with its warm white color. When you think of white as a texture, do you imagine lightness? White foods usually feel feathery and bright—airy Pavlova with Vanilla Cream, White Dragon Fruit, and Nectarines (page 36) is puffy as a cloud—but they certainly don't have to be, and it can be fun to play with this assumption. White-fleshed fish like cod is flaky and light until you poach it in coconut milk, which cloaks the fish and adds a dense creaminess (see Pickled Daikon and Coconut Cod Rice Bowls, page 28).

YELLOW
/

Smiley faces, sunflowers, school buses, rubber ducks, golden hour. Is there a happier color than yellow? Our emotions are closely linked to colors, and just seeing yellow can brighten your mood. Seeing *and* eating a happy color with a bright flavor is doubly powerful. Yellow is plentiful and easy to find at the farmers market or grocery store: egg yolks, turmeric, mustard, corn on the cob, pineapples, mangoes, lemons. Many different shades of sunny yellow are available without any culinary manipulation required. Turmeric, a rhizome related to ginger, is particularly potent as a natural food coloring—you may even have the stains on your wooden cutting boards and spoons to prove it. Turmeric is also unique in its ability to retain its vibrant hue even when baked, sautéed, or otherwise heated, and it doesn't shift color when exposed to an acidic ingredient. You'll find turmeric in more than a few of the recipes in the yellow section. It's used in savory dishes like Turmeric-

Pickled Egg Salad (page 56) as well as in sweet dishes like the Lemon Turmeric Cake with Mango Blossom (page 62). Eggs also appear regularly in this section. When egg whites and yolks are combined and baked into a Chanterelle Frittata (page 48), the dish's final color is pale yellow. When whole eggs plus a few extra yolks are used to make the lemon-lime curd for the Margarita Bars (page 50), the yellow color is more saturated. An egg yolk's precise color— which can range anywhere from light yellow to deep orange—depends almost entirely on the diet of the hen who laid that egg. If the eggs were laid by hens that ate copious amounts of yellow-orange pigments called xanthophylls, the color of the yolks will fall on the deep orange side of the spectrum. Xanthophylls belong to a class of pigments called carotenoids that are responsible for yellows, oranges, and reds. Some plants have high levels of carotenoids, but their characteristic warm yellow color is obscured by even higher levels of chlorophyll (the green pigment that is essential for photosynthesis). For instance, green grass contains tons of carotenoids, which is why grass-fed cows produce creamy, yellow-tinted milk and why traditionally made cheddar cheese is orange.

ORANGE
/

In painting, if you mix red pigment with yellow pigment, you create orange. But it's not so simple when you're color cooking. A few recipes in this section do employ a modified color-mixing strategy to achieve an orange hue (such as the gochujang sour cream that goes with Sweet Potato Rösti (page 74) and the harissa yogurt sauce for Ribboned Carrots (page 76), both of which are made from an orange-red combined with white, creating a pale orange). But most recipes in this section rely on fruits and vegetables that are orange to begin with: October pumpkins, persimmons, kumquats, nasturtium blossoms, butternut squash, sweet potatoes, carrots, apricots, and, of course, oranges. Orange as a name for the fruit came about before *orange* was used as a word to describe the eye-catching color. Indigenous to southern China and mentioned in Chinese literature as early as 314 BCE, oranges spread west to Persia (where they were called *nāranj*) and India (*nāranga* in Sanskrit), and finally, more than a century after first being cultivated, they were called *oranges* by English speakers. Orange is one of the loudest colors. It shouts at you, "Hey, look at me!" Brands such as Reese's, Nickelodeon, and Mastercard utilize orange's eye-catching character. Some of the orange recipes do indeed have flashy flavors (like the Habanero Cara Cara Salmon Poke, page 78), while others are quieter and more understated. Saffron-Tangerine Frozen Yogurt (page 68) has a soft orange color and tastes creative, unique, vibrant, and invigorating without needing to holler.

RED
/

There's a duality of rawness and ripeness in red. Red is a color we immediately associate with certain flavors. Chile pepper red can be fiery. The darker red of a Bing cherry tastes deep and sweet. If given the choice at the market between a plump, ruby-red tomato and one that's still green, we reach for the ripe one because we know it's going to taste better. Red is juicy, meaty, romantic, and full of passion, but it can also signify aggression and anger. It

seems only fitting then that many red foods are spicy and often have plenty of umami. Cooking with red foods requires a keen understanding of how red pigments behave in the kitchen. Heat alters color. So does adding acidic ingredients. Raw red cabbage appears purple-red due to the presence of pigments called anthocyanins. These are the same pigments that give strawberries their red hue. Anthocyanins are water soluble, so they will leach out if submerged in water. That's why cabbage tints the water it's boiled in (see page 18). But there's another class of pigments called carotenoids that can give red color (as well as orange and yellow) to foods. Lycopene is one type of carotenoid, notable for the redness of tomatoes, grapefruit, and watermelon. If you're trying to make a dish even redder, adding more of a red ingredient may seem obvious, but it isn't always the best plan. It can be tempting to simply put lots of chile powder into a dish like chicken tikka masala to achieve a bright red, but you'll just end up with a flaming-hot sauce. Luckily, many varieties of pepper, with varying levels of heat, can add red to a dish. For example, if you use dried Kashmiri chile peppers to make chicken tikka masala (page 88), the dish will have a deep red color and won't taste overly spicy because the chiles are mild despite their intense hue. Sometimes, the key to amplifying redness comes from bringing together multiple harmonious red ingredients, as in Wine-Poached Pears with Sour Cherry Cream and Roses (page 102). Perhaps the most well-known red ingredient is the beet, infamous for its ability to stain countertops and aprons alike. Beets do make an appearance in the red section (Beets, Blood Oranges, and Radicchio, page 104), but as it turns out, they are more useful as a natural pink food coloring.

PINK
/

Pink is somewhat elusive in the kitchen. Naturally red ingredients like strawberries and tomatoes are easier to find, and purple foods like ube and purple cauliflower, though less common, are still available at farmers markets and specialty grocery stores. Some ingredients have a pink part (such as the innermost layers of shallots), and some dishes have what you might call a "pink moment," when they turn rosy for a brief time, like Slow-Roasted Harissa Salmon (page 112). When you are able to achieve a tone like the neon hot pink of Chilled Summer Borscht (page 126), it feels like hitting a home run. Pink foods are spunky, fun, and playful and can range in color from the deeply saturated tones in a dish like Beet-Balls with Pickled Turnip Dip (page 124) to the pale pink of ballerina slippers in Spanish-Style Garlic Shrimp (page 118). One of the greatest delights in the kitchen occurs when you're expecting a food to look a certain way but it surprises you. Have you ever sliced a green-skinned watermelon radish, expecting it to be white inside, only to find its fuchsia interior? It'll take your breath away. When you follow pink recipes, you'll learn to spot the perfectly pink shade of medium-rare in Pomegranate-Sumac Lamb (page 120). You'll marvel at the way beet juice imbues gravlax with the colors of a tropical sunset. You might fall in love with pink peppercorns, which are milder and a little sweeter than black peppercorns. Pink salt might win you over, too. Produced most famously in Hawaii and the Himalayas, pink salt is tinged a rosy hue thanks to trace minerals. The saltiness can vary quite a lot, depending on the variety you're using. For these recipes, pink salt is mostly used as a finishing touch, and has the added benefit of being visible on the plate rather than dissolved into the food.

PURPLE
/

Purple is the color of royalty, power, luxury, and opulence. Purple also has a connection to the psychedelic sixties: think purple concert posters and tie-dyed shirts, Jimi Hendrix's "Purple Haze," Austin Powers in a velvet purple striped suit. Purple foods might feel mysterious, unexpected, even sacred to many. They are among the trickiest to cook because anthocyanins, the pigments responsible for purple tones, are prone to changing color when heated or combined with other ingredients. For instance, blueberries are blue by name, and they do indeed have a deep ocean color to their skin, but as soon as you cut one in half, you'll notice that they are green inside. If you cook blueberries and sugar into jam, they transform to a distinct purple shade. Freeze-dried blueberries give Blueberry-Cherry Amaretti (page 142) their majestic color. You can see the color-shifting effect that acidic lemon juice has on purple cauliflower when you make Cauliflower Rice with Red Orach (page 144). The cauliflower is chopped finely in a food processor until it resembles rice, cooked in a skillet for a few minutes, and then drizzled with fresh lemon juice. The low pH of the lemon juice instantly turns the cauliflower a more vibrant red-purple color, as if by magic. Purple recipes also present an opportunity to upend traditions. You can start with a classic recipe like pumpkin pie and reinvent it as Purple Sweet Potato Pie Bars with Cornmeal Crust (page 136).

BLUE
/

Naturally occurring blue, like the cloudless sky on a sunny day, is the rarest color in fruits and vegetables. But it does exist in some edible flower petals like bachelor's button, borage, and butterfly pea, and the effect is nothing short of mesmerizing. Butterfly pea flower is a fascinating blue ingredient. It lends its hue to many of the recipes in this section, but you should be aware that it is a color-shifting ingredient (see page 18). Dried butterfly pea flowers steeped in boiling water will dye the water deep blue. But as soon as an acidic ingredient like lemon juice is introduced, the water will turn purple. Fish skin can also look blue, with a beautiful iridescent sheen. And let's not forget about the blue-green algae called spirulina. What does blue taste like? Blue foods do have something of a shocking

quality to them, probably because they are so rare. We have a biological aversion to foods that could be harmful, like blue molds, so many of us might initially look askance at blue bread or blue dough. Sky Dumplings (page 164) are shaped and pleated with care. Blue Jean Easter Egg Breads (page 158) are adorned with a blue-dyed egg. There's no question that these foods are meant to be blue. The Ombré Crêpe Cake (page 160) is inspired by a mathematical equation, the Weber-Fechner law. Visual perception is not always as straightforward as it looks. If you want your crêpe cake to appear to transition from white to blue in ten even steps, you'll need to use a geometric progression, adding twice as much to the second crêpe, four times as much to the third crêpe, eight times as much to the fourth, and so on. This is because an increase of one unit of color is very easy to perceive if the crêpe has no blue in it. It's much harder for our eyes to detect that one extra

unit of blue if the crêpe already has ten units of blue in it! Blue foods are special and playful, and they teach us that what we see isn't always what we expect to taste.

GREEN

/

Green is growth, abundance, the color of nature, health, money, and luck. Fresh herbs like cilantro, basil, parsley, and mint are slightly different shades of saturated green. Obviously, lettuces and salad greens are green but so are fennel bulbs, fava beans, tiny French Le Puy lentils, and slender green beans. Pistachio is a green nut and lime is a green fruit. Matcha, a finely powdered green tea, can be used in the kitchen as a natural food coloring. It lends its verdant color to both Matcha-Lime Teacake (page 176) and Matcha and Mint Ice Cream Sundae (page 170). Green foods are common, and so it can

be a challenge to come up with ideas that feel new and a little surprising. For example, take a classic Caesar salad, which is traditionally green only from romaine lettuce, and transform it into a green-on-green-on-green version: Little Gem Caesar with Spinach Croutons (page 172). How can the croutons be made to be green? (Cook them like garlic bread spread generously with spinach-dyed butter.) Can the dressing be green, too? Yes! Every recipe in this section has been pushed one step further in the green direction. Some of the flavor combinations might sound unexpected, but give them a shot and you'll discover new loves like the happy harmony of apple and fennel. When cooking green foods, remember that chlorophyll (the green pigment found in every plant) is an oil-soluble pigment. You already know this if you've ever made pesto— when you chop fresh basil finely and mix it with olive oil, the green from the herb leaves is drawn out by the oil and dyes the oil an even greener color. But, if you were to briefly boil fresh basil leaves, the water wouldn't turn green. And if you use a dull knife to chop that fresh basil, the blade will just bruise the herb rather than slice through it, and you'll end up with a brownish hue. Brown foods are beautiful, but that's not the shade you're aiming for with pesto, and if you want brown, there are better ways to get there!

BROWN
/

Few dishes are more appetizing to gaze at than Piri-Piri Chicken and Potatoes (page 196) or a platter of Slow-Roasted Guajillo Pork (page 200) or steaming-hot Brown Butter Gnocchi with Wild Mushrooms and Bread Crumbs (page 194). Aside from their gorgeous shades of amber, ochre, and hickory, brown foods are incredibly delicious. Brown tastes burnished, caramelized, cooked over fire. What could be better? Brown foods don't need to be disguised with garnishes of different colors; they are beautiful and complete just as they are. The dark brown recipes in this section, like Mocha Cake with Ganache Frosting (page 202), will make your mouth water, and the light brown recipes like Parsnip Soup with Toasted Sunflower Seeds and Dates (page 190) are calming. Tonal shades of beige soothe us and give comfort. In terms of culinary techniques to learn from brown recipes, the greatest one is that cooking with relatively high heat (plus the right amount of moisture and time) causes the Maillard reaction, a chemical process involving amino acids and reducing sugars that gives browned foods their distinctive colors, aromas, and flavors. Imagine the crackly crust of a loaf of bread, the char of a grilled steak or burger, the robust smell of brewed coffee. These are all tasty results of the Maillard reaction. The recipes

in this section rely on both browning foods (as in the Caramelized Onion and Anchovy Tart on page 198) and on using beautiful brown ingredients like dates, pinto beans, and cumin seeds.

BLACK
/

Black foods are sophisticated, elegant, and dignified. They command authority. They are simultaneously formal and mysterious. They have serious style. The recipes in this section rely on ingredients like cocoa noir powder, black tahini, and squid ink, all of which give their spectacular darkness to black foods. There are a couple of notable color-theory practices you can borrow from the art world to create black dishes. The first, the Bezold effect, is an optical illusion whereby a color's appearance will change depending on the colors surrounding it. For example, black Forbidden Rice looks even darker when rolled inside a sheet of inky-hued nori (page 216). Placing a dark ingredient next to another one will amplify the darkness of each one. Some black recipes in this section take inspiration from the oil-painting technique called Pointillism that artists like Georges Seurat mastered in the Postimpressionist era. Tiny dots of colored paint are applied close together on the canvas, and the viewer's eye and brain blend the colors to create a fuller range of tones and half-tones. The colors in the photographs of this book you're holding are reproduced using a similar technique—by placing thousands of ink dots in varying density on the page. For the recipes in this section, small seeds like chia and black sesame essentially function as flecks of color. Chia Puddings with Blackberries (page 220) have a speckled appearance, neither white nor black but rather somewhere in between. As a cook, you also become a painter.

PICKLED DAIKON AND COCONUT COD RICE BOWLS

Serves 4

¾ cup (180 ml) rice vinegar
1 tablespoon plus 1 teaspoon sugar
Fine sea salt
3¾ cups (900 ml) water
8 ounces (225 g) daikon radish, peeled and thinly sliced
2 cups (400 g) uncooked short-grain white rice, rinsed
4 (6-ounce/170 g) ling cod or other white-fleshed fish fillets
Freshly ground white pepper
2 tablespoons vegetable oil
1 large shallot, thinly sliced
4 garlic cloves, thinly sliced
1 (3-inch/7.5 cm) piece fresh ginger, peeled and cut into matchsticks
2 (13.5-ounce/400 ml) cans full-fat coconut milk
Juice of 2 limes
White sesame seeds, for garnish

In a small nonreactive pot, combine the vinegar, 1 tablespoon of the sugar, 1½ teaspoons salt, and ¾ cup (180 ml) of the water. Bring to a boil. Add the daikon slices, remove the pot from the heat, and let the daikon pickle in the pot until cool, about 1 hour.

Bring the remaining 3 cups (720 ml) water to a boil in a medium saucepan. Add the rice and 1 teaspoon salt. Decrease the heat to medium-low, cover the pot, and cook for 18 minutes, until all the water has been absorbed. Remove the lid, fluff the rice with a fork, then cover and allow the rice to rest off the heat for 10 minutes.

Meanwhile, sprinkle the fish with salt and white pepper on both sides. Warm the vegetable oil in a large sauté pan over medium heat. Add the shallot, garlic, and ginger and cook, stirring, until softened but not yet browned, 2 to 3 minutes. Pour in the coconut milk and bring to a gentle simmer. Place the fish in the pan, cover, leaving the lid slightly ajar, and cook until flaky and opaque in the center, about 7 minutes. (You may need to poach the fish in two batches if the fillets are large.)

Use a spatula to transfer the fish to a plate. Bring the liquid in the pan to a boil and stir in the lime juice and remaining 1 teaspoon sugar. Cook until slightly thickened, about 5 minutes. (For a completely white presentation, strain the sauce.)

Spoon some steamed rice into each serving bowl. Tile the pickled daikon slices on top of the rice, overlapping them slightly like the shingles on a house. Top with a cod fillet, drizzle with a spoonful of the coconut sauce, and sprinkle with white sesame seeds.

/

Thin slices of pickled daikon, tiled over a bed of steamed rice, are a crunchy contrast to the creamy coconut milk–poached cod.

CHICKEN-JICAMA SALAD WITH CUMIN CREMA

Serves 4 to 6

½ small jicama (about
    10 ounces/285 g)
1 roasted or rotisserie
    chicken breast (about
    6 ounces/170 g), chopped
1 teaspoon cumin seeds
¼ cup crema (30 g) or crème
    fraîche (60 g)
1 tablespoon fresh lime juice
Fine sea salt
¼ small white cabbage, cored
1 lime, cut in half
Salty white crackers,
    for serving

Peel the jicama, cut it into matchsticks, and place in a medium bowl. Add the chicken.

In a small dry skillet, toast the cumin seeds over medium heat until fragrant and a shade darker, 2 to 3 minutes. Using a mortar and pestle or a spice grinder, grind the toasted seeds to a powder.

In a small bowl, stir together the crema, lime juice, ¼ teaspoon salt, and the ground cumin. Add the cumin crema to the bowl with the jicama and chicken and mix gently until evenly coated.

Slice the cabbage into ribbons as thin as you can possibly make them. Arrange the cabbage on serving plates, sprinkle with a pinch of salt, and squeeze the cut lime halves over the top. Spoon the chicken-jicama salad onto the cabbage. Serve with salty crackers.

/

A warm, welcoming shade of white, like a thick wool sweater or the paint color you might choose for a cozy living room.

WEDDING GOWN CUPCAKES

Makes 12 cupcakes

Cupcakes
1½ cups (180 g) cake flour
2 teaspoons baking powder
½ teaspoon fine sea salt
½ cup (1 stick/115 g)
    unsalted butter, at room
    temperature
1 cup (200 g) granulated sugar
3 large egg whites
1 teaspoon pure almond
    extract
½ cup (120 ml) whole milk

Buttercream
½ cup (1 stick/115 g)
    unsalted butter, at room
    temperature
1½ cups (190 g) confectioners'
    sugar
¼ teaspoon pure almond
    extract
Pinch of fine sea salt
2 to 3 tablespoons heavy
    cream

Make the cupcakes: Preheat the oven to 350°F (175°C). Line a 12-well cupcake pan with paper liners.

In a small bowl, whisk together the flour, baking powder, and salt.

In the bowl of a stand mixer fitted with the paddle attachment, beat the butter and granulated sugar on medium-high speed until light and fluffy, 3 to 5 minutes. Add the egg whites and almond extract and mix on medium-high speed until fully incorporated, about 1 minute. Add one-third of the flour mixture and half the milk. Mix on low speed to combine, then add another third of the flour mixture and the remaining milk. Mix on low speed for just a few seconds. Add the last of the flour mixture and mix until just barely incorporated.

Divide the batter evenly among the wells of the prepared pan, filling each about three-quarters full. Bake until the cupcakes are springy when pressed lightly and a toothpick inserted into the center comes out without any wet batter clinging to it, about 18 minutes. Transfer the cupcakes to a wire rack and let cool.

Make the buttercream: In the bowl of a stand mixer fitted with the paddle attachment, beat the butter on medium-high speed until fluffy, 3 to 5 minutes. With the mixer running, gradually add the confectioners' sugar and beat until incorporated. Add the almond extract, salt, and 2 tablespoons of the cream. Mix on medium speed for 1 minute. If you'd like the buttercream to be a bit looser, mix in the remaining 1 tablespoon cream.

Spread or pipe a generous dollop of buttercream on top of each cooled cupcake.

/

Using egg whites only (no yolks) and almond extract (rather than the darker vanilla extract) makes these cupcakes as light as can be, although the oven does kiss them with the barest golden tint. Pipe the fluffy frosting like pleats on a satin gown or thick folds of velvet.

32

RADISH, BELGIAN ENDIVE, AND RICOTTA SALATA

Serves 4 to 6

4 large Belgian endives
1 large bunch white radishes
    (about 10 small)
Fine sea salt
Freshly ground white pepper
1 small garlic clove, peeled
Juice of 1 lemon
2 tablespoons extra-virgin
    olive oil
1 tablespoon crème fraîche
2 ounces (57 g) ricotta salata
    cheese, very thinly sliced

Trim the bottoms of the endives and gently separate the leaves, trimming a bit more off the bottom as needed to detach the inner leaves. Slice the radishes as thinly as possible. Layer the endive and radish on a large serving plate. Season with ¼ teaspoon salt and lots of white pepper.

Using a mortar and pestle, pound the garlic and a pinch of salt to a smooth paste. Stir in the lemon juice, olive oil, and crème fraîche. Drizzle the dressing over the endive and radish and scatter the ricotta salata over the top.

/

A trio of airy, light-colored ingredients come together in this elegant salad. Crème fraîche makes the dressing appropriately opaque—you can substitute labne or Greek yogurt, if you like.

34

PAVLOVA WITH VANILLA CREAM, WHITE DRAGON FRUIT, AND NECTARINES

Serves 6

4 large egg whites
Pinch of fine sea salt
1 cup (200 g) granulated sugar
2 teaspoons cornstarch, sifted
1 teaspoon white wine vinegar
½ teaspoon pure vanilla
   extract
2 cups (480 ml) heavy cream
1 tablespoon confectioners'
   sugar
1 vanilla bean
1 white dragon fruit, scooped
   with a melon baller
2 large or 3 small white
   nectarines, pitted and cut
   into thin wedges
Dried coconut flakes, for
   sprinkling

Preheat the oven to 350°F (175°C). Using a pencil, trace a 9-inch (23 cm) circle on a piece of parchment paper, then flip the paper over and place it on a baking sheet.

In the bowl of a stand mixer fitted with the whisk attachment, combine the egg whites and salt. Beat on high speed for 1 minute. With the mixer running on high, gradually add the granulated sugar and beat until shiny, stiff peaks form, 2 to 3 minutes. Use a rubber spatula to gently fold in the cornstarch, vinegar, and vanilla. Transfer the mixture to the prepared parchment paper, smoothing it out into a round disc and using the circle as a guide. Place in the oven, immediately lower the oven temperature to 300°F (150°C), and bake until crisp on the outside but still soft inside, 1 hour 15 minutes. Turn off the oven and leave the meringue inside with the door closed until completely cool.

Just before serving, peel off the parchment paper and place the meringue on a serving platter. Use the back of a wooden spoon to gently crack the meringue in a few places.

In a medium bowl, combine the cream and confectioners' sugar. Cut the vanilla bean in half lengthwise and scrape all the tiny black seeds into the cream. Whip until the cream holds soft peaks, then spread it across the meringue. Top with the dragon fruit and nectarines. Garnish with coconut flakes.

/

If a puffy cloud or a mound of untouched snow could be turned into a showstopping dessert, pavlova would be it. Topped with white dragon fruit and nectarines (or your favorite white fruit), it's best shared and eaten the day it's made.

CHICKEN CONGEE

Serves 4

6 cups (1.4 L) water
2 pounds (910 g) bone-in,
  skin-on chicken thighs
¾ cup (150 g) uncooked
  short-grain white rice,
  rinsed
1 tablespoon finely grated
  fresh ginger
4 scallions, white parts only,
  thinly sliced
Fine sea salt
Sesame oil, for garnish
Cracked white pepper

In a large heavy-bottomed pot, combine the water and chicken. Bring to a gentle simmer, cover the pot, leaving the lid ajar, and cook, stirring occasionally, until the chicken is cooked through, about 15 minutes. Use tongs to transfer the chicken to a plate, leaving the broth in the pot. Chop or shred the meat into bite-size pieces, discarding any bones. Cover the chicken and refrigerate until ready to serve.

Add the rice to the broth in the pot and cook at a gentle simmer, stirring every 15 minutes or so, until the grains burst and the congee thickens to the consistency of oatmeal, about 1½ hours. Stir in the ginger, scallions, and half the cooked chicken. (Save the rest of the chicken for another recipe.) Taste and season with salt. Serve the chicken congee garnished with a drizzle of sesame oil and freshly cracked white pepper.

/

Ginger and chicken broth both impart a hint of goldenness. It's pure comfort in a bowl.

TZATZIKI COUSCOUS

Serves 6

1 small yellow onion,
    finely chopped
5 tablespoons (75 ml)
    extra-virgin olive oil
2½ cups (600 ml) vegetable
    broth or water
Fine sea salt
1½ cups (225 g) dried pearl
    (Israeli) couscous
1 large English cucumber
    (about 14 ounces/400 g),
    grated on the large holes
    of a box grater
1 (15-ounce/425 g) can
    chickpeas, drained and
    rinsed
1½ cups (430 g) plain
    whole-milk Greek yogurt
2 tablespoons very finely
    chopped fresh dill
2 tablespoons very finely
    chopped fresh mint
1 tablespoon preserved lemon
    paste or minced preserved
    lemon

In a medium saucepan, cook the onion in 3 tablespoons of the olive oil over medium heat, stirring occasionally, until softened but not at all browned, about 3 minutes. Pour in the broth and bring to a boil. Season with salt—you want it well seasoned to flavor the couscous (½ teaspoon salt is about right if you use water; use a little less salt if you use broth). Add the couscous and bring the broth back up to a simmer, then decrease the heat to low and cover the pot. Cook until the couscous is tender and has absorbed most of the liquid, about 10 minutes.

Meanwhile, working with one big handful at a time, squeeze the grated cucumber over the sink to remove excess water. Place the squeezed cucumber in a large serving bowl. Add the chickpeas, yogurt, dill, mint, preserved lemon paste, and remaining 2 tablespoons olive oil. Mix well.

When the couscous is done, drain off any remaining liquid, then stir the couscous into the cucumber-yogurt mixture.

/

Tzatziki, a yogurt-based sauce, cloaks pearl couscous and chickpeas in this hearty vegetarian dish. Be sure to chop the fresh herbs as finely as possible so that they are just tiny flecks of color, barely perceptible.

RICE NOODLES WITH CREAMY TOFU SAUCE

Serves 4

7 ounces (200 g) soft silken
    tofu
2 tablespoons rice vinegar
2 teaspoons toasted sesame
    oil, plus more for tossing
1 tablespoon white miso paste
2 garlic cloves, peeled
½ teaspoon fine sea salt
14 ounces (400 g) fresh thin
    rice noodles (vermicelli) or
    7 ounces (200 g) dried
1 bunch scallions, white parts
    only, very thinly sliced on a
    diagonal
3 tablespoons white sesame
    seeds
½ cup (75 g) cashews, toasted
    and chopped

Place the tofu, vinegar, sesame oil, miso, garlic, and salt in a blender and blend until smooth and creamy.

Bring a large pot of water to a boil. Add the rice noodles to the water, use tongs to make sure they're all submerged, and then immediately turn off the heat under the pot. Stir the noodles occasionally until they are tender but still a little chewy in a pleasant way, 5 to 10 minutes. Drain and rinse under cold water. Transfer the noodles to a large bowl. (If you're not saucing them right away, toss them with a little sesame oil to prevent them from sticking to each other.)

Pour the tofu sauce over the noodles and mix well. Scatter the scallions, sesame seeds, and cashews over the top and serve.

/

Pure white soft silken tofu, blended into a creamy sauce, is tinted ever so slightly and nudged in the direction of yellow by miso paste and toasted sesame oil.

PITA, CHAMOMILE-STEEPED BURRATA, AND HAWAIIAN HONEY

Serves 4 to 6

Burrata

½ cup (120 ml) olive oil
2 tablespoons dried chamomile
    flowers
3 garlic cloves, thinly sliced
1 teaspoon whole white
    peppercorns
1 strip of lemon peel (use a
    vegetable peeler)
2 teaspoons white wine
    vinegar
1 or 2 (8-ounce/225 g) balls
    burrata cheese

Pita

1 cup (240 ml) lukewarm water
1 (¼-ounce/7 g) packet dry
    yeast (2¼ teaspoons)
1 teaspoon sugar
2¾ cups (350 g) all-purpose
    flour, plus more for shaping
1 tablespoon olive oil, plus
    more for the bowl
1 teaspoon fine sea salt

⅓ cup (115 g) Kiawe honey,
    gently warmed until
    pourable
Fresh chamomile petals, for
    garnish

/

Hawaiian kiawe honey naturally crystallizes to a pearly white hue and tastes like tropical flowers. Here, it is paired with pale golden pita and creamy burrata cheese that has been marinated in chamomile oil.

Prepare the burrata: In a small saucepan, combine the olive oil, dried chamomile, garlic, and white peppercorns and heat over medium-low heat. Let the garlic fizzle gently for 3 to 4 minutes, then remove from the heat. Stir in the lemon peel and vinegar and let cool completely.

Place the burrata in a shallow bowl. Pour in the chamomile oil. Cover and refrigerate for at least 1 hour or up to 2 days.

Meanwhile, make the pita: In a medium bowl or liquid measuring cup, combine the warm water, yeast, and sugar. Stir to dissolve the sugar, then set aside until the mixture is foamy, about 5 minutes.

Put the flour, olive oil, and salt in the bowl of a stand mixer fitted with the dough hook. Pour in the yeast mixture and mix on medium speed, pausing and scraping down the sides of the bowl as needed, until a sticky dough comes together. Increase the speed to medium-high and knead the dough until it's smooth and elastic, about 7 minutes. Oil a large bowl and transfer the dough to the bowl. Cover with a clean kitchen towel and let rise until doubled in size, about 1 hour.

Divide the dough into 6 equal pieces, roll each piece into a ball, and place them all on a floured work surface. Cover with the same kitchen towel and let rest for 20 minutes.

Place a baking sheet in the oven and preheat the oven to 500°F (260°C).

Working with one dough ball at a time, roll it out to a circle about 5 inches (12.5 cm) in diameter. Be careful not to create any little rips in the dough. Use a spatula or your hands to carefully transfer the rolled dough to the preheated baking sheet in the oven. Immediately close the oven door and bake until the pita puffs, about 4 minutes. Repeat to roll out and bake the other dough balls, doing two at a time, if you want. Stack the baked pita breads on a plate and cover with a clean kitchen towel to keep them soft.

Transfer the burrata to a serving bowl large enough for a snug fit. Drizzle with a little of the marinating oil (reserve the remaining oil in an airtight container in the refrigerator for salad dressing or another recipe) and all the honey. Garnish with the chamomile petals and serve with the warm pita alongside.

GARLICKY GIGANTE BEANS, SALT-AND-VIN CAULIFLOWER, AND PINE NUTS

Serves 4 to 6

2 cups (400 g) dried gigante
    beans
1 yellow onion
6 garlic cloves, smashed and
    peeled
⅓ cup (80 ml) plus
    2 tablespoons extra-virgin
    olive oil, plus more for
    drizzling
1 large head white cauliflower,
    cut into bite-size florets
Fine sea salt
Freshly ground white pepper
⅓ cup (45 g) pine nuts
2 tablespoons white wine
    vinegar

/

**Three different off-white
shades—toasted pine nuts,
roasted cauliflower, and
brothy beans—combine to
create a speckled, terrazzo-
like effect.**

Place the beans in a large heavy-bottomed pot. Add enough water to cover by about 2 inches (5 cm). Cut the onion in half, peel away the papery skin, and drop the halves into the pot. Add the garlic cloves to the pot along with 2 tablespoons of the olive oil.

Bring the water to a lively boil and cook for 10 minutes, then lower the heat so the liquid barely simmers. Partially cover the pot and cook until the beans are completely soft all the way through, 1½ to 2 hours total, depending on the age of the beans. Every so often, uncover the pot, give the beans a stir, and check the water level. If the beans are poking out, add more hot water to submerge them.

Meanwhile, preheat the oven to 500°F (260°C).

In a large bowl, toss the cauliflower with the remaining ⅓ cup (80 ml) olive oil. Season with salt and white pepper.

Heat a large oven-safe skillet over high heat for 1 minute. Transfer the cauliflower to the skillet and cook, stirring only once or twice, for about 5 minutes, until golden brown in a few places. Transfer the skillet to the oven and roast the cauliflower for 5 minutes, or until brown in a few more places. Stir in the pine nuts, then roast for 3 minutes more, or until the cauliflower is just tender. Remove from the oven.

When the beans are tender, stir in 1 teaspoon salt, wait a few minutes, then taste a bean and a sip of broth. Season with more salt, knowing that only the broth will taste salty at first and then the beans will slowly absorb the salt. Fish out and discard the onion halves.

Transfer the cauliflower to a shallow serving bowl, drizzle with the vinegar, and mix. Using a slotted spoon, add the beans to the bowl and mix very gently. Top with a drizzle of olive oil and serve warm.

CHANTERELLE FRITTATA

Serves 6

12 large eggs
½ cup (120 g) crème fraîche
½ cup (55 g) grated
    semi-firm cheese, such as
    Jarlsberg or Fontina
2 tablespoons extra-virgin
    olive oil
Fine sea salt
4 tablespoons (½ stick/57 g)
    unsalted butter
8 ounces (225 g) chanterelle
    mushrooms, cleaned and
    torn into bite-size pieces
4 garlic cloves, thinly sliced

Preheat the oven to 300°F (150°C).

In a large bowl, combine the eggs, crème fraîche, cheese, olive oil, and 1 teaspoon salt. Whisk until just combined.

In a 12-inch (30 cm) oven-safe skillet, melt the butter over medium-high heat. When the butter starts to foam, add the mushrooms and a pinch of salt and stir them around in the pan, then cook, without stirring, until golden brown on the undersides, 3 to 5 minutes. Stir and cook until tender and golden brown all over, 3 to 5 minutes more. Add the garlic and cook, stirring often, for 1 more minute. Pour in the egg mixture. Stir with a wooden spoon for 90 seconds, then transfer the skillet to the oven and bake until the frittata is just barely set in the center but still a little jiggly, about 20 minutes. Let the frittata cool for a few minutes before serving.

/

A pale, eggy yellow is made a bit lighter with crème fraîche and grated cheese. The mushrooms are golden, scattered about. You can use yellow oyster mushrooms or any other light-colored mushroom you prefer, but earthy chanterelles really do shine in this frittata.

MARGARITA BARS

Makes 16 bars

1½ cups (190 g) all-purpose flour
¼ cup (30 g) confectioners' sugar
¼ teaspoon fine sea salt
½ cup (1 stick/115 g) unsalted butter, melted, plus 6 tablespoons (¾ stick/ 85 g), cut into cubes, at room temperature
6 limes
2 lemons
1½ cups (300 g) granulated sugar
2 large eggs
3 large egg yolks
2 teaspoons cornstarch
2 tablespoons tequila
1 tablespoon Grand Marnier
1 Meyer lemon, cut into paper-thin half-moon slices and seeded
Flaky sea salt, for sprinkling

Preheat the oven to 325°F (165°C). Line an 8-inch (20 cm) square baking pan with parchment paper.

In a medium bowl, stir together the flour, confectioners' sugar, and fine salt. Mix in the melted butter. Transfer the mixture to the prepared pan and press it evenly over the bottom to create a flat crust with no gaps. Bake until golden brown, about 30 minutes. Keep the oven on.

Meanwhile, finely grate 1 tablespoon of zest from the limes and set the zest aside, then squeeze the limes and lemons to get ¾ cup (180 ml) juice total. In a medium saucepan, combine the citrus juices, granulated sugar, eggs, egg yolks, and cornstarch. Bring to a boil over medium heat, whisking continuously. Strain through a fine-mesh sieve into a medium bowl. Whisk in the room-temperature butter, tequila, Grand Marnier, and lime zest.

Pour the lime filling over the baked crust. Bake until the filling is set around the edges but still a little wobbly in the center, 30 to 35 minutes. Let cool to room temperature, then cover loosely and refrigerate until completely chilled. Cut into bars, place a slice of Meyer lemon on each bar, sprinkle with flaky salt, and serve.

/

These may look like classic lemon bars, but they taste like a margarita, with a boozy whiff of tequila and extra brightness from fresh lime. Meyer lemons are sweeter and less acidic than regular lemons, so they are the ideal garnish, along with a nonnegotiable pinch of salt.

NEW POTATO SALAD WITH CREAMY MUSTARD AND GARLIC CHIPS

Serves 4 to 6

Fine sea salt
1¾ pounds (795 g) baby yellow
    potatoes, peeled and cut
    into bite-size pieces
½ cup (120 ml) olive oil
7 garlic cloves, thinly sliced
⅓ cup (80 g) crème fraîche
2 tablespoons Dijon mustard
2 tablespoons whole-grain
    mustard
2 tablespoons apple cider
    vinegar

Bring a pot of generously salted water to a boil. Add the potatoes and cook until tender when poked with a fork, about 15 minutes.

Meanwhile, in a small saucepan, heat the olive oil over medium heat. Add the garlic and fry, stirring often, until lightly golden. Immediately pour the garlic and oil through a fine-mesh sieve into a bowl. Transfer the garlic chips to a paper towel to drain.

In a large bowl, stir together the crème fraîche, Dijon mustard, whole-grain mustard, vinegar, and 2 tablespoons of the garlic oil. (Reserve the remaining garlic oil in an airtight container at room temperature for another purpose.)

When the potatoes are done cooking, drain them and transfer directly to the bowl with the mustard sauce. Toss gently to coat. Taste and season with more salt, if needed. Sprinkle with the garlic chips and serve warm or at room temperature.

/

Yellow potatoes dressed in mustard sauce and sprinkled with crisp garlic chips. This is the golden boy of picnic fare.

PINEAPPLE CHICKEN SATAY WITH SUNSHINE SAUCE

Serves 6

2 lemongrass stalks
1 (13.5-ounce/400 ml) can
    full-fat coconut milk
¼ cup (85 g) honey
¼ cup (60 ml) fresh lime juice
1 shallot, chopped
3 garlic cloves, chopped
1 (2-inch/5 cm) piece fresh
    ginger, peeled and chopped
1 tablespoon ground turmeric
1 tablespoon vegetable oil
¼ cup (70 g) tahini
Fine sea salt
1½ pounds (680 g) boneless,
    skinless chicken thighs, cut
    into 1-inch (2.5 cm) pieces
1 pineapple, peeled, cored, and
    cut into ½-inch (1.5 cm)
    cubes

Soak eighteen 6-inch (15 cm) bamboo skewers in cool water for at least 15 minutes. Line a rimmed baking sheet with aluminum foil.

Meanwhile, trim off and discard all but the bottom few inches of the lemongrass stalks. Peel away the tough green layers until you reach the softer purple-white interior. Chop this coarsely and place it in a small saucepan. Pour in the coconut milk and bring to a boil, then remove from the heat and let steep for 10 minutes.

Transfer the lemongrass–coconut milk to a blender and add the honey, lime juice, shallot, garlic, ginger, turmeric, and vegetable oil. Blend until smooth. Pour all but about ½ cup (120 ml) of the mixture into a large bowl. Add the tahini to the aromatic mixture remaining in the blender and blend until smooth. Taste the sauce and season with salt, then set aside for serving.

Add the chicken, pineapple, and 1 teaspoon salt to the aromatic mixture in the large bowl and mix well. Cover and let marinate at room temperature for 30 minutes or in the refrigerator for up to 2 days.

Heat a charcoal grill or oven broiler to high. Thread the chicken and pineapple onto the skewers, alternating chicken and pineapple, and place the skewers on the prepared baking sheet. Discard the marinade. Grill or place under the broiler until the chicken is cooked through, 5 to 10 minutes per side. Serve with the sunshine sauce for dipping.

/

Bottled sunshine—in the form of a honeyed, spiced sauce. Half of the sauce is used to marinate chicken and pineapple, and the other half becomes a dip for the satay. To make a vegetarian version, simply swap the meat for extra-firm tofu cubes.

TURMERIC-PICKLED EGG SALAD

Serves 4

¾ cup (180 ml) apple cider
    vinegar
¾ cup (180 ml) water
1 tablespoon sugar
2 teaspoons ground turmeric
1 teaspoon fine sea salt
6 large eggs
3 tablespoons mayonnaise
1½ teaspoons yellow mustard
Yellow curry paste, for dabbing
4 slices of bread

In a 1-quart (1 L) jar, stir together the vinegar, water, sugar, turmeric, and salt. Set aside.

Fill a large bowl with ice and water and set it nearby. Fill a nonreactive (i.e., *not* aluminum, cast iron, or unlined copper) medium pot halfway with water and bring to a boil. Carefully lower in the eggs, adjust the heat so that the water simmers gently, and cook for exactly 8 minutes. Transfer the cooked eggs to the bowl of ice water and let cool for 2 minutes, then crack and peel away the shells.

Place the peeled eggs in the jar with the turmeric pickling brine, cover, and refrigerate for at least 1 hour and up to 3 days.

Chop the pickled eggs and place them in a medium bowl. Add the mayonnaise, mustard, and 1 tablespoon of the egg-pickling brine. Mix well.

To serve, dab some curry paste on the bread, then top with the egg salad.

/

This one looks as if someone turned up the yellow dial on egg salad. Yolks get a boost in color from turmeric, and a smidge of yellow curry paste spread on the bread hides beneath the egg salad, waiting to surprise you.

UDON IN SPICY COCONUT BROTH

Serves 2 to 4

2 tablespoons vegetable oil
2 tablespoons sesame oil
1 large yellow onion, chopped
3 garlic cloves, thinly sliced
1 (2-inch/5 cm) piece fresh
    ginger, peeled and finely
    grated
Fine sea salt
2 small fresh Thai chiles, or
    1 habanero, stemmed and
    finely chopped
1 tablespoon yellow curry
    paste
2 teaspoons ground turmeric
1 (13.5-ounce/400 ml) can
    full-fat coconut milk
2 cups (480 ml) vegetable
    broth
1 pound (450 g) fresh or frozen
    udon noodles
2 tablespoons fresh lime juice

In a large pot, warm the vegetable oil and sesame oil over medium heat. Add the onion, garlic, ginger, and ½ teaspoon salt. Cook, stirring often, until the onion softens and turns translucent, about 5 minutes. Mix in the chiles, curry paste, and turmeric and cook for 2 minutes. Pour in the coconut milk and broth and bring to a boil. Cook, stirring occasionally, until slightly thickened, 30 to 40 minutes. Taste and season with more salt, if needed.

Meanwhile, bring a large pot of water to a boil. Add the udon noodles and cook as directed on the package, until al dente. Drain.

Just before you're ready to serve, stir the cooked noodles and lime juice into the coconut broth. Taste and season with more salt as needed.

/

Yellow, yellow, and more yellow—sesame oil, yellow onion, garlic and ginger, yellow curry paste, and turmeric all add their sunny hues to this dish.

ROASTED SUMMER SQUASH BRUSCHETTA

Serves 4 to 6

1¼ pounds (565 g) yellow
    summer squash, cut into
    ½-inch (1.5 cm) cubes
Extra-virgin olive oil
Fine sea salt
Freshly ground white pepper
1 large piece of focaccia
½ lemon
1 cup (245 g) fresh whole-milk
    ricotta
Fennel pollen, for garnish

Preheat the oven to 400°F (200°C). Line a baking sheet with parchment paper.

Put the squash on the baking sheet, drizzle with 3 tablespoons olive oil, and sprinkle with ½ teaspoon salt and lots of white pepper. Use your hands to toss the squash around until it's evenly coated in the oil, then spread out the squash pieces into a single layer with some space around each cube. Roast until the squash is tender and golden brown in a few places, 30 minutes.

Meanwhile, slice the focaccia horizontally into two large pieces like the top and bottom buns of a giant hamburger. Brush both cut sides generously with olive oil. Place them in the oven cut-side up, directly on the rack, and toast until lightly crisp.

When the squash is done roasting, squeeze some lemon juice over it. Spread the ricotta over the toasted bread. Pile the squash on top of the ricotta, sprinkle with fennel pollen, and serve.

/

A flourish of fennel pollen is what makes this dish sparkle. Fennel pollen isn't cheap, but you only need a pinch or two. Think of it as decorative gold leaf—only much zestier and tastier.

LEMON TURMERIC CAKE WITH MANGO BLOSSOM

Serves 8

Unsalted butter, for the pan
1½ cups (190 g) all-purpose
　　flour
2 teaspoons baking powder
2 teaspoons ground turmeric
½ teaspoon fine sea salt
1 cup (200 g) sugar
2 lemons
½ cup (120 g) plain whole-milk
　　Greek yogurt
2 large eggs
½ cup (120 ml) neutral-
　　flavored oil, such as canola
　　or safflower
3 tablespoons tropical blossom
　　honey
1 teaspoon orange blossom
　　water
1 large ripe mango
1 tablespoon bee pollen,
　　for garnish

/

This spectacular cake will
impress your friends. The sliced
mango blossom on top is no
doubt the scene-stealer, but
the cake itself is also vibrantly
yellow.

Preheat the oven to 350°F (175°C). Generously butter a round 8-inch (20 cm) cake pan and line the bottom with parchment paper cut to fit.

In a medium bowl, whisk together the flour, baking powder, turmeric, and salt.

Measure the sugar into a large bowl. Use a rasp grater to zest the lemons directly into the bowl of sugar (reserve the zested lemons). Using your fingertips, pinch and rub the zest into the sugar until the sugar is pale yellow and fragrant. Add the yogurt and eggs. Whisk vigorously until smooth. Add the flour mixture and whisk until there are no visible streaks of flour. Use a rubber spatula to fold in the oil. Scrape the batter into the prepared pan and smooth the top. Bake until the cake springs back when lightly pressed and a toothpick inserted into the center comes out clean, about 35 minutes.

Meanwhile, squeeze 3 tablespoons of juice from the zested lemons into a small saucepan. Add the honey and warm gently over medium-low heat. As soon as the mixture bubbles, swirl the pan to dissolve the honey, then remove from the heat and add the orange blossom water.

Let the cake cool in the pan for about 5 minutes, then spoon half the honey syrup over the top. Let the syrup soak in for a few minutes before inverting the cake onto a wire rack, turning it right-side up, and letting it cool completely.

Peel the mango and slice downward along the hard central pit to form a flat-sided "cheek." Turn the mango 90 degrees and cut another cheek. Repeat twice more to cut 4 cheeks total, then thinly slice each cheek. Arrange the mango slices on top of the cake in slightly overlapping concentric circles like petals on a flower, leaving a 1-inch (2.5 cm) circle in the middle bare. Brush the remaining honey syrup over the mango and sprinkle the bee pollen into the circle.

PRESERVED LEMON RICOTTA AGNOLOTTI

Serves 4 to 6

1 preserved lemon
1 lemon
1½ cups (370 g) fresh whole-milk ricotta cheese
¼ cup (25 g) finely grated Parmigiano-Reggiano cheese
Freshly ground black pepper
Semolina flour, for dusting
12 ounces (340 g) pre-rolled fresh pasta sheets
4 tablespoons (½ stick/57 g) unsalted butter

Use a spoon to scrape out and discard the squishy flesh of the preserved lemon. Finely chop the peel. Place half the chopped peel in a small bowl and set aside the other half for the sauce.

Zest the fresh lemon and add the zest to the bowl with the chopped preserved lemon (set the zested lemon aside). Add the ricotta, Parmigiano, and a few grinds of pepper and stir to combine.

Lightly dust a baking sheet with semolina.

Lay one sheet of fresh pasta on a clean work surface. Spoon heaped teaspoons of the lemony ricotta along one long edge of the pasta sheet, about 2 inches (5 cm) in from the edge, spacing them ¾ inch (2 cm) apart from each other. Brush the area around each mound of filling with water, then fold the pasta sheet lengthwise over the filling and press gently to seal and squeeze out the air. Use a fluted pasta cutter to cut along the top of the row and then in between each mound to create individual agnolotti. Place them on the prepared baking sheet. Repeat with the remaining pasta sheets and filling.

Bring a large pot of generously salted water to a boil.

In a large sauté pan, melt the butter over medium-high heat. Let the butter brown, then add the remaining preserved lemon. Juice the zested fresh lemon into the pan.

When the water boils, add the agnolotti and cook until just barely tender, about 2 minutes. Use a slotted spoon to transfer them directly to the pan of sauce. Stir in ¼ cup (60 ml) of the pasta cooking water. Increase the heat to medium-high and cook, shaking the pan gently, until the sauce thickens slightly and coats the pasta, 2 to 3 minutes.

/

Like tiny satchels of gold coins, these delicate pouches are filled with lemony ricotta, and a butter sauce balances and smooths the salty, tart citrus flavors.

BANANA PEPPER AND CORN SALAD

Serves 4

2 ears fresh yellow corn,
    shucked
3 tablespoons unsalted butter
4 scallions, white parts only,
    thinly sliced
2 garlic cloves, thinly sliced
3 fresh banana peppers, seeds
    and ribs removed, sliced
    crosswise into ¼-inch-wide
    (6 mm) strips
½ teaspoon fine sea salt
Zest and juice of 1 to 2 limes

Stand one corncob upright in a bowl, with the fatter end up. Cut downward along the cob with a sharp knife, pressing the blade along the cob and collecting all the kernels in the bowl. Repeat with the second ear of corn.

In a large skillet, melt the butter over medium-high heat. Add the scallions, garlic, and banana peppers. Season with the salt and cook, stirring occasionally, until the scallions and garlic soften, 3 minutes. Add the corn kernels and a splash of water and cook, stirring, for 2 minutes. Remove the pan from the heat. Stir in half the lime zest and juice. Taste and add the remaining lime zest and juice, if you'd like it to be a little more tart. Serve warm.

/

Banana peppers are the color of—you guessed it—bananas. The two also share a similar shape. You can use any bright yellow pepper for this summery salad, but make sure to choose yellow corn rather than white corn to achieve the intended cheerful hue.

SAFFRON-TANGERINE FROZEN YOGURT

Makes about 1 quart (1 L)
frozen yogurt

2 cups (570 g) plain whole-milk
Greek yogurt
1½ teaspoons bitter red liqueur
(such as Aperol)
Pinch of fine sea salt
¼ cup (50 g) sugar
Finely grated zest of
2 tangerines
¼ cup (60 ml) fresh tangerine
juice
2 tablespoons honey
Pinch of saffron
¾ cup (180 ml) whole milk

In a large bowl, stir together the yogurt, liqueur, and salt until combined.

In a small saucepan, combine the sugar and tangerine zest. Using your fingers, pinch and rub the zest into the sugar until the mixture turns orange and smells fragrant. Add the tangerine juice to the pan. Bring to a boil, then cook, stirring to dissolve the sugar, until the liquid has reduced in volume by half, about 5 minutes. Remove the pan from the heat, stir in the honey and saffron, and set aside to cool for 1 minute.

Whisk the cooled tangerine syrup and the milk into the yogurt mixture. Cover and refrigerate the yogurt base until completely chilled, at least 3 hours.

Transfer the chilled yogurt base to an ice cream maker and churn according to the manufacturer's instructions. You can serve right from the ice cream maker or you can transfer the frozen yogurt to a freezer-safe container, press a piece of parchment paper directly against the surface of the yogurt, cover tightly with the lid, and store in the back of the freezer for a few hours if you want it to be firmer. Before serving, let the frozen yogurt warm up for a few minutes at room temperature until scoopable.

/

Saffron and tangerine are a match made in heaven. Their flavor profiles are similar: sweet, heady, floral, a bit musky. They lend their orange hues to this frozen yogurt, which is easy to make and even easier to eat.

BAKED MACARONI AND SQUASH

Serves 8

1 medium butternut squash
   (about 2 pounds/910 g)
3 cups (720 ml) whole milk
1 sprig sage
Fine sea salt
1 pound (450 g) dried pasta
   shells or elbows
1½ cups (170 g) grated sharp
   cheddar cheese
½ cup (55 g) grated pecorino
   cheese
Freshly ground black pepper

Preheat the oven to 325°F (165°C).

Peel and seed the squash, then cut the flesh into ¾-inch (2 cm) cubes. Place the squash cubes in a medium saucepan. Add the milk, sage, and 1 teaspoon salt and bring to a simmer. Partially cover the pot and cook until the squash is tender when poked with a fork, 15 to 20 minutes.

Meanwhile, bring a pot of generously salted water to a boil. Add the pasta and cook until not quite al dente, about 5 minutes. Drain and set aside.

When the squash is done, fish out and discard the sage, then use an immersion blender to purée the squash and milk to make a smooth sauce. Stir in the pasta, cheddar, pecorino, and lots of pepper. Mix well, then transfer to a large oven-safe dish. Bake until hot and bubbling, 15 to 20 minutes. Continue baking for 10 minutes more if you'd like the top to be a little crispy.

/

Butternut squash's deep orange color uplifts the cheddar cheese in this baked pasta, and the squash's soft creaminess adds lushness, too.

SUNGOLD TOMATO GAZPACHO

Serves 4 to 6

½ small red onion, peeled
2 or 3 Persian cucumbers,
    peeled
1 large orange bell pepper,
    seeds and ribs removed
1½ pounds (680 g) Sungold
    tomatoes (from about
    2 pint baskets), stemmed
1 garlic clove, peeled
2 teaspoons sherry vinegar
Pinch of red pepper flakes
1 teaspoon fine sea salt
⅓ cup (80 ml) olive oil, plus
    more for drizzling

Chop the onion, cucumbers, and bell pepper into 1-inch (2.5 cm) pieces and put them in a blender. Set aside a large handful of the tomatoes for serving and add the rest to the blender along with the garlic, vinegar, red pepper flakes, and salt. Blend on high speed for 2 minutes, or until very smooth.

With the blender running, slowly drizzle in the olive oil. The mixture will lighten in color and thicken a little bit to the consistency of salad dressing. Strain the gazpacho through a fine-mesh sieve into a large bowl; discard the solids. Cover the soup and chill it in the refrigerator for at least 1 hour or up to 3 days.

Just before serving, cut the reserved tomatoes in half and season them with a big pinch of salt. Serve the gazpacho in small bowls or tall frosty glasses, topped with the tomato halves and drizzled with olive oil.

/

The name of this tomato says it all: Sungold. It's a color that tastes energetic, spirited, and dynamic. Use an orange bell pepper, if you can find one, or half of a red pepper and half of a yellow.

SWEET POTATO RÖSTI WITH GOCHUJANG SOUR CREAM

Serves 4 to 6

4 small or 2 large sweet
    potatoes (about
    2 pounds/910 g)
1½ teaspoons fine sea salt
1 cup (225 g) sour cream
1 tablespoon gochujang
½ cup (75 g) kimchi, drained
    and very finely chopped
2 large eggs
1 tablespoon cornstarch
¼ cup (60 ml) vegetable oil
Gochugaru, for garnish

Preheat the oven to 425°F (220°C).

Peel and coarsely grate the sweet potatoes using a box grater. In a large bowl, toss the grated sweet potato with the salt and let rest for about 5 minutes.

Meanwhile, in a small serving bowl, stir together the sour cream and gochujang. Refrigerate until ready to serve.

Working in batches, firmly squeeze fist-sized amounts of the salted, grated sweet potato, pressing out and discarding the liquid. Mix the kimchi, eggs, and cornstarch into the squeezed sweet potatoes.

Heat the vegetable oil in a large oven-safe skillet over medium-high heat for 1 minute. Add the sweet potato mixture to the pan and use a spatula to spread it out almost all the way to the edge of the pan into a giant pancake about ½ inch (1.5 cm) thick. Transfer to the oven and roast until the bottom and edges are browned but the top is still vibrant orange, about 30 minutes.

Bring the rösti to the table in the pan it was cooked in and serve the bowl of gochujang sour cream alongside. Garnish with a sprinkle of gochugaru.

/

A combination of sweet potatoes and kimchi makes this rösti as orange as a basketball. The sour cream garnish presents another opportunity to bring more color to the dish, in this case by mixing in some gochujang.

RIBBONED CARROTS ON HARISSA YOGURT

Serves 6 to 8

6 large carrots (about
    2½ pounds/1.1 kg)
2 teaspoons cumin seeds
1 tablespoon ground turmeric
Zest and juice of 1 small
    orange
¼ cup (60 ml) plus 1 tablespoon
    olive oil
Fine sea salt and freshly
    ground black pepper
¾ cup (185 g) plain whole-milk
    yogurt
1 tablespoon harissa

Fill your largest bowl with ice and water. Use a vegetable peeler to make long ribbonlike strips of carrot. (The best way to create wide ribbons is to place the carrot on a cutting board, hold it securely on one end, and run the peeler along the length of the carrot while pressing down firmly. Repeat until you're left with long, floppy bits from the center of the carrot—use them in soups and stocks.) Soak the carrot ribbons in the ice water until they become slightly crunchier, about 5 minutes.

Meanwhile, in a small dry pan, toast the cumin seeds over medium heat until they turn a shade darker and smell fragrant. Transfer the cumin to a large bowl and stir in the turmeric, orange zest, 2 tablespoons of the orange juice, ¼ cup (60 ml) of the olive oil, 1 teaspoon salt, and several grinds of pepper. Drain the carrot ribbons and transfer them to the bowl with the spice mixture. Toss to coat.

In a small bowl, stir together the yogurt, harissa, 1 tablespoon of the orange juice, and the remaining 1 tablespoon olive oil. Season with salt and pepper. Spoon the harissa yogurt onto a serving platter, coil and arrange the carrot ribbons on top of the yogurt, and serve.

/

You can use a humble vegetable peeler to transform carrots into edible ribbons. Coil the ribbons and arrange them upright on the plate so that the harissa yogurt is visible underneath.

HABANERO CARA CARA SALMON POKE

Serves 4 to 6

12 ounces (340 g) sashimi-
   grade boneless, skinless
   salmon fillet
2 Cara Cara oranges
¼ sweet Maui or Vidalia onion,
   very thinly sliced or finely
   chopped
1 habanero pepper, stemmed
   and very thinly sliced
1 tablespoon soy sauce or
   tamari
2 teaspoons honey
2 teaspoons toasted sesame oil
¼ teaspoon fine sea salt
Steamed rice, for serving

Using a sharp knife, cut the salmon with the grain into ½-inch-thick (1.5 cm) slices, then cut each slice crosswise into ½-inch (1.5 cm) cubes and place them in a large bowl.

Cut the top and bottom off one orange. Stand the orange on one cut side on your cutting board so that it doesn't roll around. Place the blade of your knife at the top of the orange and cut down, tracing the curved line of the fruit, to remove a section of the peel and white pith. Rotate the orange and continue cutting away the peel and pith until you've removed it all. Go back and trim any pith still clinging to the fruit. Hold the orange in your nondominant hand over the bowl and use the tip of the knife to free each little segment of fruit, slicing on either side of the white membrane between each segment to release them. Repeat with the second orange. Once you've cut out all the segments, squeeze the membrane that's left behind to get about ¼ cup (60 ml) orange juice. Add the segments and the collected juice to the bowl with the salmon.

Add the onion, habanero, soy sauce, honey, sesame oil, and salt. Gently mix. Let stand at room temperature for about 5 minutes before serving with steamed rice.

/

Raw salmon is almost identical in color to Cara Cara orange segments. Seek out sweet Cara Caras both for their striking color and because they are ideal for poke—seedless and low in acidity, they separate cleanly from the rind.

PERSIMMON-KUMQUAT SALAD WITH GOJI DRESSING AND NASTURTIUMS

Serves 4 to 6 (makes
1¾ cups/420 ml dressing)

¼ cup (20 g) dried goji berries
¼ cup (60 ml) rice vinegar
2 large carrots, coarsely grated
1 (2-inch/5 cm) piece fresh
    ginger, peeled and finely
    grated
3 tablespoons fresh lime juice
1 tablespoon honey
Fine sea salt
6 tablespoons (90 ml)
    extra-virgin olive oil
1 tablespoon toasted sesame
    oil
3 Fuyu persimmons, peeled
2 cups (370 g) kumquats
⅓ cup (35 g) pecans, toasted
    and chopped
Handful fresh nasturtium
    flowers

Place the goji berries in a blender. In a small saucepan, warm the vinegar until it's nearly boiling, then pour it over the goji berries and let them soak for about 5 minutes. Add the carrots, ginger, lime juice, honey, and ½ teaspoon salt. Blend on high speed for 1 minute. With the blender running on low speed, gradually add the olive oil and sesame oil, then blend on high speed for 1 minute.

Core the persimmons, slice them into ¼-inch-thick (6 mm) rounds, and place them in a shallow bowl. Thinly slice the kumquats into ⅛-inch-thick (3 mm) rounds and remove the seeds. Add the kumquats to the bowl with the persimmons. Season with a pinch of salt. Drizzle with about ½ cup (120 ml) of the dressing and use your hands to toss gently until the fruits are evenly coated. Toss with more dressing, if you like.

Spread a spoonful of dressing in an arc on each serving plate. Arrange the dressed fruits on top, scatter the pecans and nasturtium flowers, and serve.

/

At the tail end of persimmon season, kumquats appear in markets. The two share the same eye-catching hue and taste gorgeous together in this salad.

SPICY KABOCHA TEMPURA

Serves 4 to 6

2 quarts (2 L) vegetable oil,
    for frying
1 small kabocha squash (about
    3 pounds/1.4 kg)
1 cup (125 g) all-purpose flour
1 cup (110 g) cornstarch
2 teaspoons shichimi togarashi
2 teaspoons fine sea salt
1½ cups (360 ml) chilled
    sparkling water

Pour the vegetable oil into a heavy pot and heat to 375°F (190°C). Line a baking sheet with a wire rack, a layer of paper towels, or a clean brown paper bag.

Peel the squash, then carefully cut it in half and remove the stem and seeds. Cut the squash into ¼-inch-thick (6 mm) slices.

In a large bowl, combine the flour, cornstarch, shichimi togarashi, and salt. Pour in the sparkling water and whisk until just barely incorporated.

When the oil is ready, dip 6 or so slices of the squash in the batter and then carefully lower them into the hot oil. Fry, stirring with chopsticks or a wire-mesh strainer, until crisp and golden, 2 to 5 minutes. Transfer the tempura squash to the prepared baking sheet and repeat to cook the remaining squash. Serve hot.

/

Shichimi togarashi, a Japanese spice mixture containing seven ingredients (including dried orange peel), gives this tempura a subtle and nuanced spiciness.

PUMPKIN PANCAKES

Serves 3 or 4

1½ cups (190 g) all-purpose
   flour
2 tablespoons sugar
1½ teaspoons baking powder
¾ teaspoon baking soda
2 teaspoons pumpkin pie spice
½ teaspoon fine sea salt
¼ teaspoon ground turmeric
Mounded ¾ cup (210 g) canned
   pumpkin purée (half a
   15-ounce/425 g can)
1 cup (240 ml) whole milk
1 large egg
4 tablespoons (½ stick/57 g)
   unsalted butter, melted
   and cooled slightly, plus
   more at room temperature
   for the pan
Pure maple syrup, warmed,
   for serving

In a medium bowl, whisk together the flour, sugar, baking powder, baking soda, pumpkin pie spice, salt, and turmeric.

In another bowl, whisk together the pumpkin, milk, egg, and melted butter until completely smooth. Pour the pumpkin mixture into the flour mixture and whisk gently until just combined.

Heat a large skillet over low to medium-low heat. Add a small piece of butter and let it melt, swirling the pan to lightly coat. Spoon ⅓ cup (80 ml) of the batter into the pan and cook until many tiny bubbles form on the surface, about 3 minutes. Flip and cook on the second side until the pancake is cooked through, about 2 minutes. Transfer to a warm plate and repeat with the remaining batter. Stack the pancakes and serve hot, drizzled generously with warm maple syrup.

/

Orange pumpkin tends to turn brown when it's spiced with a mix of cinnamon, ginger, and cloves and cooked. (Picture a baked pumpkin pie.) But if you add just a little bit of ground turmeric—not enough that you'll taste it—the orange color gets amplified.

APRICOT JAM TART

Makes one 9-inch (23 cm) tart

1 cup (125 g) all-purpose flour
1 cup (100 g) almond flour
¼ teaspoon fine sea salt
½ cup (1 stick/115 g)
 unsalted butter, at room
 temperature, plus more for
 the pan
⅓ cup (65 g) sugar
Finely grated zest of 1 lemon
Juice of ½ lemon
1 (8-ounce/250 g) jar
 apricot jam

Preheat the oven to 350°F (175°C). Line the bottom of a 9-inch (23 cm) fluted round tart pan with parchment paper cut to fit.

In a large bowl, mix together the all-purpose flour, almond flour, and salt.

In another large bowl, use a wooden spoon to beat the butter, sugar, and lemon zest until creamy and lightened in color, about 3 minutes. (Alternatively, you can use a stand mixer and beat with the paddle attachment on medium-high speed.) Add the flour mixture and mix slowly until incorporated.

Press the dough into an even layer over the bottom and up the sides of the prepared pan. Empty the jam into a small bowl and stir in the lemon juice. Spread the jam mixture evenly over the dough. Bake until the crust is golden brown, about 40 minutes. Let cool before serving.

/

Bright apricot orange, with a hint of rosiness.

KASHMIRI CHILE CHICKEN TIKKA MASALA

Serves 4 to 6

3 tablespoons Kashmiri chile
   powder, plus more for
   sprinkling
2 tablespoons cumin seeds,
   toasted
2 teaspoons garam masala
2 teaspoons ground turmeric
6 garlic cloves, finely grated
1 (2-inch/5 cm) piece fresh
   ginger, peeled and finely
   grated
1½ cups (375 g) plain
   whole-milk yogurt
¼ cup (60 ml) fresh lemon juice
Fine sea salt
2 pounds (910 g) boneless,
   skinless chicken thighs or
   breasts, cut into 1-inch
   (2.5 cm) pieces
3 tablespoons ghee or unsalted
   butter
1 yellow onion, thinly sliced
¼ cup (55 g) tomato paste
2 dried chiles de árbol,
   stemmed
1 (28-ounce/794 g) can whole
   peeled tomatoes
1½ cups (360 ml) heavy cream
Steamed jasmine rice, for
   serving

/

Kashmiri chile powder is
the reddest of them all but
thankfully doesn't taste as
flaming-hot as it looks.

In a small bowl, stir together the Kashmiri chile powder, cumin seeds, garam masala, and turmeric. Transfer half the spice mixture to a large bowl and set the remainder aside.

Add the garlic, ginger, yogurt, lemon juice, and 1 tablespoon salt to the large bowl with the spice mixture. Mix well. Add the chicken, stirring to coat it in the marinade. Cover and refrigerate for 4 to 6 hours.

In a Dutch oven, melt the ghee over medium-high heat. Add the onion, tomato paste, and chiles de árbol and cook, stirring, until the onion softens, about 5 minutes. Stir in the reserved spice mixture and cook for about 1 minute. Add the can of tomatoes and simmer, stirring occasionally, until the sauce thickens, about 15 minutes. Use an immersion blender to purée the sauce directly in the pot. Stir in the cream, season with salt, and keep warm over very low heat.

Preheat the broiler to high. Line a rimmed baking sheet with aluminum foil.

Remove the chicken from the marinade, wipe off excess marinade, and place on the prepared baking sheet. Broil until charred in a few places but not yet cooked through, about 10 minutes. Transfer the broiled chicken to the sauce and bring to a simmer. Cook, stirring often, until the chicken is cooked through, 5 minutes. Sprinkle with a pinch of Kashmiri chile powder for even more vibrant red color and serve over steamed rice.

CHERRY TOMATO AGRODOLCE WITH 'NDUJA ON TOAST

Serves 6

2 pints (600 g) red cherry
    tomatoes
6 anchovies
6 Calabrian hot peppers
¼ cup (60 ml) extra-virgin
    olive oil
3 tablespoons red wine vinegar
2 tablespoons honey
Fine sea salt and freshly
    ground black pepper
6 slices country-style bread
2 ounces (57 g) 'nduja

Preheat the oven to 300°F (150°C).

Place the cherry tomatoes in a roasting dish large enough to accommodate them snugly, piled up on top of each other here and there. Drape the anchovies over the tomatoes and scatter the Calabrian peppers on top. Drizzle the olive oil, vinegar, and honey over everything and season with salt and black pepper. Roast, stirring once or twice, until the tomatoes collapse into a jammy sauce.

Toast the bread, spread it thickly with 'nduja from edge to edge so you can't see any bread, and top with a big spoonful of the tomato agrodolce.

/

When a red tomato cooks,
a distinct shift in color
happens—it moves in the
direction of orange, like it
went on vacation and came
back home a little bronzed.

MAPO RAGÙ WITH RICE CAKES

Serves 4 to 6

2 yellow onions, sliced
3 tablespoons vegetable oil
Fine sea salt
1 pound (450 g) ground pork
2 pounds (910 g) garaetteok
   (cylindrical Korean rice
   cakes)
3 garlic cloves, thinly sliced
1 (2-inch/5 cm) piece fresh
   ginger, peeled and finely
   grated
4 scallions, white and green
   parts kept separate, thinly
   sliced
1 tablespoon sesame oil
3 tablespoons gochujang
1 tablespoon soy sauce or
   tamari
½ teaspoon whole Sichuan
   peppercorns
1 tablespoon gochugaru

In a large skillet, cook the onions in the vegetable oil over medium heat, stirring occasionally at first and then more frequently, until golden brown and lightly caramelized, about 30 minutes. Season with ¼ teaspoon salt and transfer to a medium bowl (set the skillet aside).

Bring a large pot of salted water to a boil.

In the same skillet you used for the onions, cook the pork over medium-high heat, stirring and using a wooden spoon to break up the meat into crumbles, until cooked through, 8 to 10 minutes. Transfer to the bowl with the caramelized onions (set the skillet aside again).

When the water boils, add the rice cakes and cook until not quite tender, 2 to 3 minutes. Scoop out and reserve 1 cup (240 ml) of the cooking water, then drain the rice cakes in a colander.

In the same skillet you used for the pork, cook the garlic, ginger, and the white parts of the scallions in the sesame oil over medium heat, stirring continuously, until fragrant and softened but not yet browned, about 2 minutes. Add the gochujang, soy sauce, Sichuan peppercorns, reserved 1 cup (240 ml) cooking water, and the caramelized onions and pork. Bring to a simmer, stirring to combine. Mix in the rice cakes and the green parts of the scallions, sprinkle with the gochugaru, and serve right away.

/

These chewy rice cakes are doused in a meaty sauce that's stained red by gochujang. To amplify the red color of this dish even further, sprinkle generously with gochugaru (Korean chile powder) before serving.

TOMATO TART

Makes one 12-inch (30 cm) tart

1½ cups (190 g) all-purpose flour, plus more for rolling
1 tablespoon sugar
Fine sea salt
¾ cup (1½ sticks/170 g) unsalted butter, sliced and chilled
⅓ cup (80 ml) ice-cold water
1½ pounds (680 g) red heirloom tomatoes, sliced ¼ inch (6 mm) thick
3 tablespoons grated Parmigiano-Reggiano cheese

In a large bowl, stir together the flour, sugar, and ¾ teaspoon salt. Using your fingertips, rub the butter into the flour mixture until the butter pieces are the size of corn kernels. Pour in the water and quickly but gently knead until a ball of dough comes together. Wrap the dough in plastic wrap and refrigerate for at least 1 hour or up to 3 days.

Preheat the oven to 375°F (190°C). Line a rimmed baking sheet with parchment paper.

In a colander set over a bowl, gently toss the tomatoes and 1 teaspoon salt. Set aside to drain for 5 minutes, until the salt has drawn out some of the tomato juices. Carefully transfer the tomato slices to paper towels to drain a little more. Discard the juices in the bowl.

On a lightly floured surface, roll out the dough into a large round or oval about ⅛ inch (3 mm) thick. Place the dough on the prepared baking sheet. Scatter the cheese evenly over the dough and arrange the tomato slices on top of the cheese, leaving a 1-inch (2.5 cm) border around the edge. Fold the exposed dough over the tomatoes. Chill in the refrigerator (or, even better, the freezer—if it will fit!) for 10 minutes.

Bake the tart, rotating the pan once, until the crust is dark golden brown, about 70 minutes.

/

You can use one variety of tomato for this tart to achieve a uniform color. Or, try a combination of a few varieties that are all slightly different shades of red—they'll blend together visually to create a unique hue.

COPPA-WRAPPED JIMMY NARDELLOS

Serves 4

2 tablespoons extra-virgin
  olive oil
14 ounces (400 g) Jimmy
  Nardello peppers (about 24),
  stemmed
1½ teaspoons red wine vinegar
½ teaspoon ground sumac
Flaky sea salt
4 ounces (115 g) thinly sliced
  coppa

Heat a large cast-iron skillet over medium-high heat for 1 minute. Add the olive oil and peppers to the hot skillet, stir to coat the peppers in the oil, and cook, without stirring, for 3 minutes, or until the peppers are dark brown in a few places. Cook, stirring only once or twice, until the peppers are tender and collapse a little bit from the heat, 4 to 7 minutes. When you lift a pepper with tongs and it droops slightly, it's done; if it stays rigid, cook it for 1 more minute or so. Transfer to a wide, shallow serving dish or plate.

Drizzle the vinegar over the peppers and sprinkle with the sumac. Season generously with a few big pinches of flaky salt. Pick up one large or two small peppers and wrap with a slice of coppa. Secure with a toothpick, if you like. Repeat with the remaining peppers. Serve warm.

/

An optical illusion of sorts, this dish with its devil's horn–shaped peppers looks like it would taste fiery. But the chiles are surprisingly sweeter than a bell pepper.

STRAWBERRY MILKSHAKE PANCAKES

Serves 3 or 4

Cranberry Sauce
**12 ounces (340 g) fresh
  cranberries**
3 large blood oranges
6 tablespoons (75 g) sugar
Pinch of fine sea salt

Pancakes
**1 cup (25 g) freeze-dried
  strawberries**
**1½ cups (190 g) all-purpose
  flour**
1 tablespoon sugar
1 teaspoon red beet powder
**1 tablespoon plus ½ teaspoon
  baking powder**
¼ teaspoon fine sea salt
1 large egg
1 cup (240 ml) whole milk
**3 tablespoons unsalted
  butter, melted and cooled
  slightly, plus more at room
  temperature for the pan**
1 teaspoon pure vanilla extract

Make the cranberry sauce: Place the cranberries in a medium saucepan. Use a vegetable peeler to remove 2 strips of orange peel and drop them into the pan. Squeeze the oranges to get ¾ cup (180 ml) of juice and add that to the pan along with the sugar and salt. Bring to a simmer and cook until some but not all of the cranberries burst, 5 to 10 minutes. Remove from the heat and let cool while you make the pancakes.

Make the pancakes: Using a food processor, process the freeze-dried strawberries to a fine powder. Transfer the strawberry powder to a large bowl, add the flour, sugar, beet powder, baking powder, and salt, and whisk to combine.

Use a fork to beat the egg into the milk, then add the mixture to the bowl with the dry ingredients. Add the melted butter and vanilla and stir until just combined but with a few lumps remaining.

Heat a large nonstick pan over low heat. Melt about 1 teaspoon butter in the pan, then add ¼ cup (60 ml) of the pancake batter for each pancake, leaving space for them to spread a little. Cook until bubbles appear on the surface and the bottoms are golden, 2 to 4 minutes. Flip and cook on the second side until golden, 2 to 4 minutes. Transfer the cooked pancakes to a plate and repeat to cook the remaining batter. Serve each short stack of pancakes topped with cranberry sauce.

/

**This creamy strawberry
milkshake in pancake form
is topped with scarlet red
cranberry and blood orange
sauce.**

AHI TUNA AGUACHILE ROJO

Serves 4 to 6

12 ounces (340 g) sashimi-
grade boneless, skinless
ahi tuna fillet
Fine sea salt
½ cup (120 ml) water
¼ cup (10 g) flor de jamaica
(dried hibiscus flowers)
1 pint (290 g) strawberries,
stemmed
2 red Fresno peppers, stemmed
and seeded
1 dried chile de árbol, stemmed
and broken into pieces
¼ cup (60 ml) fresh lime juice
¼ red onion, very thinly sliced
Beet chips, or red tortilla chips
sprinkled with mild chile
powder, for serving

Holding a sharp knife at a 45-degree angle, cut the ahi tuna with the grain into ½-inch-thick (1.5 cm) slices, then cut each slice crosswise again at an angle into bite-size ½-inch-thick (1.5 cm) pieces and place them in a shallow dish. Sprinkle with salt, cover, and refrigerate for 1 to 2 hours.

Meanwhile, in a small saucepan, bring the water to a boil. Remove the pan from the heat, add the hibiscus, and let steep for 5 minutes. Strain the hibiscus tea and discard the flowers.

Thinly slice the 3 smallest strawberries and set them aside. In a blender, combine the remaining strawberries, the Fresno peppers, chile de árbol, lime juice, ¼ teaspoon salt, and the hibiscus tea. Purée until smooth.

Use the back of a spoon to spread a large spoonful of the aguachile mixture on each serving plate. Arrange some tuna pieces on top. Scatter the sliced small strawberries and the red onion over the top and serve with chips.

/

As if ahi tuna went for a delicious swim in strawberry-sweetened agua de jamaica. Beet chips definitely aren't traditional with aguachile rojo, but they are a perfect match in color. If you can't find them, substitute red tortilla chips sprinkled with mild chile powder.

WINE-POACHED PEARS WITH SOUR CHERRY CREAM AND ROSES

Serves 6

1 lemon
6 ripe but slightly firm pears
1 (750 ml) bottle red wine
1 cup (200 g) sugar
¼ cup (85 g) honey
1 cinnamon stick
3 whole cloves
1 star anise pod
1 cup (240 ml) heavy cream
2 tablespoons labne or thick
    Greek yogurt
½ teaspoon rose water
½ cup (160 g) sour cherry jam
1 cup (175 g) pomegranate
    arils
Petals from 1 organic red rose

Use a vegetable peeler to remove 3 strips of lemon peel from the lemon. Cut the lemon in half.

Peel the pears, leaving their stems (if they have any) intact. Rub the cut lemon all over the peeled pears. Place the pears in a Dutch oven or other heavy-bottomed pot. Add the wine, sugar, honey, cinnamon, cloves, star anise, and strips of lemon peel. Bring to a gentle simmer, cover the pot, and cook, turning once or twice, until the pears are tender when poked with a fork, about 30 minutes.

Transfer the pears to a bowl. Bring the poaching liquid to a rapid boil and cook, stirring occasionally, until syrupy and reduced to about 1 cup (240 ml). Pour the red wine syrup over the pears and let them soak until you're ready to serve.

Just before serving, in a medium bowl, whisk together the cream, labne, and rose water until it holds soft, billowy peaks. Gently fold in the sour cherry jam, mixing until it's almost combined but still a little swirly. Serve each pear with a dollop of sour cherry cream, a drizzle of the wine syrup, a large spoonful of pomegranate arils, and a few rose petals.

/

Romance and passion swirled together on a plate. Choose an organic rose, if possible, in case you decide to eat the garnish. Rose petals taste floral, a little earthy, and slightly sweet—sort of like a mild strawberry (the two are botanically related).

BEETS, BLOOD ORANGES, AND RADICCHIO

Serves 6 to 8

12 baby red beets (1½ to
    2 pounds/680 to 910 g)
1 small shallot, very thinly
    sliced
3 tablespoons red wine vinegar
    or sherry vinegar
Fine sea salt
4 large blood oranges
¼ cup (60 ml) olive oil
Freshly ground pink pepper
½ small radicchio, leaves cut
    into bite-size pieces

Preheat the oven to 375°F (190°C).

Rinse the beets and trim their tops and roots. Arrange the beets in a baking dish large enough to hold them in a single layer. Pour about ¼ cup (60 ml) water into the dish. Cover tightly with aluminum foil and roast until the beets are tender all the way through when pierced with a fork, about 1 hour. Remove from the oven and let cool slightly. When the beets are cool enough to handle, peel away their leathery skins. Cut the beets into wedges and place them in a large bowl.

Place the shallot, vinegar, and ¼ teaspoon salt in a small bowl and set aside to soften while you prepare the fruit.

Using a sharp knife, cut the top and bottom off one blood orange. Stand the orange on one cut side on your cutting board so that it doesn't roll around. Place the blade of your knife at the top of the orange and cut down, tracing the curved line of the fruit, to remove a section of the peel and white pith. Rotate the orange and continue cutting away the peel and pith until you've removed it all. Go back and trim any pith still clinging to the fruit. Slice the orange crosswise into thin rounds. Repeat with the remaining blood oranges.

Whisk the olive oil, ½ teaspoon salt, and a few grinds of pink pepper into the shallot-vinegar mixture. Pour this dressing over the beets, add the radicchio, and toss gently. Taste and adjust the seasoning, adding more salt or olive oil if needed. Arrange the salad on a platter, place the orange rounds on top, season with more pepper, and serve.

/

A salad the color of pinot noir, these three cool shades of red look striking together on the plate.

RED BERRY PORRIDGE WITH SUGAR PLUM COMPOTE

Serves 4

Red Berry Porridge
1½ pounds (680 g) mixed red raspberries and hulled strawberries
3 cups (720 ml) water
¼ cup (50 g) sugar
1 cup (200 g) steel-cut oats
¼ teaspoon fine sea salt

Sugar Plum Compote
8 plums (about 1¼ pounds/ 565 g), pitted and cut into ½-inch (1.5 cm) wedges
½ cup (120 ml) fresh grapefruit juice
¼ cup (50 g) sugar
Pinch of fine sea salt
1 teaspoon pure vanilla extract

Fresh red currants, for garnish

Make the porridge: In a medium saucepan, combine the berries, water, and sugar. Cook over medium heat, stirring occasionally, until the berries are completely broken down and the mixture is ruby red, about 20 minutes. Strain through a fine-mesh sieve, discarding the cooked berries. Return the strained syrup to the pot and bring to a simmer. Add the oats and salt. Cook, stirring every once in a while at first and more often toward the end, until the oats are tender, 30 minutes.

Meanwhile, make the compote: In a small pot over medium heat, combine the plums, grapefruit juice, sugar, and salt. Bring to a gentle simmer, cover the pot, and cook until the plums turn soft and have the consistency of jam, about 10 minutes. Remove from the heat and stir in the vanilla.

To serve, divide the porridge among four bowls. Spoon some compote on top and garnish with red currants.

/

This is oatmeal for someone who loves fruit and has a sweet tooth. You can swap plum jam for the compote, but the compote takes only about 10 minutes to cook.

BAVETTE WITH ROMESCO, PLUOTS, AND SHERRIED CHERRIES

Serves 2 to 4

Romesco
1 (8-ounce/250 g) jar roasted peppers, drained and rinsed
4 oil-packed sun-dried tomatoes, drained and rinsed
¼ cup (35 g) salted roasted almonds or Marcona almonds
1 garlic clove, peeled
2 teaspoons sherry vinegar
½ teaspoon smoked paprika (sweet or hot)
Pinch of red pepper flakes
Fine sea salt
¼ cup (60 ml) olive oil

1 flank steak (about 12 ounces/ 340 g)
Pink salt
Freshly ground pink peppercorns
½ cup (115 g) fresh or frozen pitted cherries
3 tablespoons sherry vinegar
4 tablespoons (60 ml) extra-virgin olive oil
2 pink pluots, pitted and cut into ½-inch-thick (1.5 cm) wedges

/

Slices of medium-rare rosy-colored steak, dotted with pluot wedges and cherries soaked in sherry vinegar, are nestled on a bed of paprika-red romesco sauce.

Make the romesco: In a food processor, process the roasted peppers, tomatoes, almonds, garlic, vinegar, paprika, red pepper flakes, and ½ teaspoon sea salt until combined. With the machine running, slowly pour in the olive oil and process until smooth, 10 to 30 seconds. Taste and season with more salt if needed and a little more red pepper flakes if you'd like the romesco to be spicier.

Use paper towels to pat the steak completely dry. Generously season both sides of the steak with pink salt and pink pepper, then let the steak rest at room temperature for at least 15 minutes.

Meanwhile, in a small pot, combine the cherries, vinegar, and a pinch of pink salt. Let warm over low heat for a few minutes, then remove from the heat and set aside to soak while you cook the steak.

Heat a large cast-iron skillet over medium-high heat for 3 to 4 minutes, until it's so hot it's nearly smoking. Swirl in 1 tablespoon of the olive oil. Place the steak in the skillet and cook until browned on the first side, about 4 minutes. Flip and cook on the second side to your preferred doneness, 3 to 5 minutes for medium-rare, depending on thickness. (If using a thermometer to check doneness, 130°F/54°C is medium-rare.) Transfer the steak to a plate and let rest for 10 minutes.

Spread the romesco thickly over a serving plate. Using a fork, stir the remaining 3 tablespoons olive oil into the sherried cherries. Slice the steak against the grain and nestle the slices in the romesco along with the pluot wedges. Drizzle any juices from the cut steak over the top, then spoon the cherries and their sauce over everything.

BEET-IMBUED GRAVLAX

Serves 12

8 ounces (225 g) red beets,
    peeled and chopped
Finely grated zest of 1 ruby red
    grapefruit
Finely grated zest of 2 blood
    oranges
1 cup (235 g) fine sea salt
½ cup (100 g) sugar
1 tablespoon whole pink
    peppercorns
1 whole skin-on side of salmon
    (about 2 pounds/910 g)

Using a food processor, process the beets, grapefruit zest, blood orange zest, salt, sugar, and pink peppercorns to a coarse paste.

Line a rimmed baking sheet with a large piece of plastic wrap and lay the salmon on the plastic. Spread half the beet paste over the salmon, then cover with another large piece of plastic wrap and flip the salmon over on the baking sheet. Remove the plastic and spread the remaining beet paste over the other side of the salmon. Cover again with the plastic, wrapping the fish tightly.

Stack a second baking sheet on top of the wrapped salmon and weigh it down with a heavy roasting dish or a few cans of tomatoes. Refrigerate for 24 hours.

Unwrap the salmon and rinse away the beet cure with cool water. Pat dry with paper towels. To serve, slice the gravlax on an angle, as thinly as possible.

/

Grated beets dye the salmon from the outside in, creating an ombré pattern. Pink citrus zest and pink peppercorns reinforce the color.

SLOW-ROASTED HARISSA SALMON AND PINK CHICORY SALAD

Serves 6

6 salmon fillets (about
    4 ounces/115 g each)
Fine sea salt
Freshly ground pink
    peppercorns
3 tablespoons harissa
1 small shallot, very thinly
    sliced
3 tablespoons red wine vinegar
    or sherry vinegar
¼ cup (60 ml) extra-virgin
    olive oil
1 large or 2 small heads pink
    radicchio (like La Rosa del
    Veneto or Rosalba) or pink-
    speckled lettuce
Ground sumac, for sprinkling

Preheat the oven to 250°F (120°C). Line a baking sheet with parchment paper.

Place the salmon skin-side down on the baking sheet. Season with salt and pink pepper. Rub the harissa into the salmon. Bake until just cooked in the center, 20 to 30 minutes, depending on thickness.

Meanwhile, place the shallot, vinegar, and a pinch of salt in a small bowl. Let soften for about 5 minutes, then whisk in the olive oil.

Separate the pink radicchio into individual leaves, tear them into bite-size pieces, and place in a large bowl. When the salmon is almost done, drizzle the leaves with the dressing and use your hands to toss gently.

Sprinkle the salmon generously with sumac. Serve warm or chilled, with the pink chicory salad on the side.

/

As salmon cooks, it transforms from orange to pink. A smear of harissa highlights the pink tones, as does a sprinkle of sumac on top and a pretty pink chicory salad alongside.

POMELO HAMACHI CRUDO

Serves 4 to 6

12 ounces (340 g) sashimi-
    grade boneless, skinless
    hamachi (yellowtail) fillet
Pink salt
1 pink pomelo
1 large pink grapefruit
1 small shallot, very thinly
    sliced
1 teaspoon finely grated
    fresh ginger
2 teaspoons rice vinegar
1 tablespoon toasted
    sesame oil

Holding a sharp knife at a 45-degree angle, cut the hamachi with the grain into ½-inch-thick (1.5 cm) slices, then cut each slice crosswise into ½-inch (1.5 cm) pieces. Place them on a lipped serving platter and sprinkle with pink salt.

Cut off the bottom and top of the pomelo and peel away the rind and spongy white pith. Use your fingers to gently remove the fruit from the surrounding membrane.

Using a sharp knife, cut off the top and bottom of the grapefruit. Stand the fruit on your cutting board on one cut side so it doesn't roll around. Place the blade of your knife at the top of the grapefruit and cut down, tracing the curved line of the fruit, to remove a section of the peel and white pith. Rotate the grapefruit and continue cutting away the peel and pith until you've removed it all. Go back and trim any pith still clinging to the fruit. Holding the grapefruit in your nondominant hand, cut along each thin white membrane to release the segments of fruit. Place the grapefruit segments in a fine-mesh sieve set over a bowl to catch the juice. Once you've cut out all the segments, squeeze the membrane over the segments to collect any remaining juice.

Arrange the pomelo and grapefruit segments on the platter with the fish.

In a small bowl, stir together 2 tablespoons of the collected grapefruit juice, the shallot, ginger, vinegar, and sesame oil. Drizzle this dressing over the fish and fruit and serve right away.

/

Despite also being known as yellowtail, hamachi has a rosy hue not unlike the colors of two citrus fruits: pink grapefruit and pink pomelo.

GUAVA-RHUBARB SORBET

Makes 1 quart (1 L) sorbet

5 ripe white guavas (about
    1 pound/450 g), chopped
    into ½-inch (1.5 cm) pieces
3 rhubarb stalks (about
    10 ounces/285 g), chopped
    into ½-inch (1.5 cm) pieces
1 cup (200 g) sugar
Juice of 1 lemon

In a medium saucepan, combine the guavas, rhubarb, sugar, and lemon juice. Bring to a simmer over medium-high heat and cook, stirring occasionally, until the rhubarb softens, 5 to 8 minutes. Transfer to a blender and purée until smooth. Strain through a fine-mesh sieve into a bowl. Cover the sorbet base and refrigerate until completely chilled, at least 4 hours.

Transfer the sorbet base to an ice cream maker and freeze according to the manufacturer's instructions. You can serve right from the ice cream maker or you can transfer the sorbet to another container and freeze for a few hours if you want it to be firmer. Before serving, let the sorbet warm up for a few minutes at room temperature until scoopable.

/

Pink guavas are a bit harder to find than white guavas, but you can imitate the color (and add a complementary flavor) by mixing the white fruit with red rhubarb.

SPANISH-STYLE GARLIC SHRIMP

Serves 2 to 4

1 pound (450 g) shell-on large
   shrimp
4 garlic cloves, thinly sliced
¾ teaspoon fine sea salt
¼ teaspoon baking soda
¼ teaspoon red pepper flakes
5 tablespoons (75 ml)
   extra-virgin olive oil
1 tablespoon sherry vinegar
Crusty bread or toast,
   for serving

In a medium bowl, mix together the shrimp, garlic, salt, baking soda, red pepper flakes, and 2 tablespoons of the olive oil until combined.

In a large nonreactive skillet, heat the remaining 3 tablespoons olive oil over high heat. Add the seasoned shrimp, spread them out in a single layer, and cook, stirring frequently, until barely cooked through, 2 to 3 minutes. Remove from the heat, stir in the vinegar, and serve hot, with crusty bread.

/

The palest pink of a ballet
slipper meets the punch of
garlic.

POMEGRANATE-SUMAC LAMB

Serves 4

3 garlic cloves, peeled and crushed to a paste

1 tablespoon plus 2 teaspoons ground sumac

3 tablespoons pomegranate concentrate, plus more for drizzling

¼ cup (60 ml) plus 1 tablespoon extra-virgin olive oil

1 lamb rib rack with 8 ribs, frenched or not (2½ to 4 pounds/1.1 to 1.8 kg)

Pink salt

Freshly ground pink peppercorns

1 small shallot, thinly sliced

½ cup (120 ml) red wine

1 cup (240 ml) good-quality beef broth

2 tablespoons unsalted butter

½ cup (90 g) pomegranate arils

/

Lamb cooked to perfectly pink doneness, with layers of pink from pomegranate arils, sumac, and wine sauce.

In a small bowl, stir together the garlic, 1 tablespoon of the sumac, 2 tablespoons of the pomegranate concentrate, and ¼ cup (60 ml) olive oil.

Score the lamb fat by making short, shallow cuts every 1 inch (2.5 cm) or so. Sprinkle the meaty and fatty parts of the lamb with pink salt and pink pepper, then rub with the pomegranate-sumac mixture. Place the lamb, fat-side up, on a rimmed baking sheet, cover, and let marinate at room temperature for 1 to 2 hours. (Alternatively, you can marinate the lamb in the refrigerator for up to 3 days and let it warm up at room temperature for 1 to 2 hours before roasting.)

About 15 minutes before you're ready to cook the lamb, preheat the oven to 450°F (230°C).

Roast the lamb for 10 minutes. Flip the lamb over, lower the oven temperature to 300°F (150°C), and continue roasting until the thickest part of the meat is 130°F/54°C (for medium-rare) on an instant-read thermometer, 10 to 20 minutes more. Transfer the lamb to a carving board or plate, cover with foil, and let rest for 15 minutes.

Meanwhile, in a small saucepan over medium heat, cook the shallot in the remaining 1 tablespoon olive oil, stirring, until softened, 2 minutes. Add the wine and cook for 1 minute, then pour in the broth and cook at a rapid boil until the sauce is thick enough to coat the back of a spoon. Remove the pan from the heat and swirl in the butter, remaining 1 tablespoon pomegranate concentrate, and remaining 2 teaspoons sumac.

Cut the rack of lamb between the rib bones into individual chops and place them on a serving platter. Drizzle the wine sauce and a little more pomegranate concentrate over the lamb and scatter the pomegranate arils.

ROSE-GLASSES FORTUNE COOKIES

Makes about 20 cookies

¼ cup (10 g) flor de jamaica
    (dried hibiscus flowers)
½ cup (120 ml) boiling water
3 large egg whites
⅔ cup (135 g) sugar
½ teaspoon rose water
¼ teaspoon fine sea salt
½ cup (1 stick/115 g) unsalted
    butter, melted and cooled
    slightly
1 cup (125 g) all-purpose flour
1 tablespoon red dragon fruit
    powder

Place the hibiscus flowers in a small bowl and pour in the boiling water. Let steep for 5 minutes, then strain the hibiscus tea through a fine-mesh sieve.

In a large bowl, whisk together the egg whites, sugar, rose water, and salt until frothy. Add the melted butter and 3 tablespoons of the hibiscus tea and stir until incorporated. Mix in the flour and dragon fruit powder. Cover and chill the batter in the refrigerator for 1 hour.

Write fortunes on 20 small strips of paper.

Preheat the oven to 350°F (175°C). Line a baking sheet with a nonstick baking mat or a piece of parchment paper. Have a coffee mug and a muffin tin nearby.

Spoon a heaping tablespoon of the batter onto the prepared baking sheet and use the back of the spoon to spread it out into a thin circle about 4 inches (10 cm) in diameter. Repeat to form another 2 cookies on the baking sheet, leaving as much space as possible among them. Bake until the cookies are just set and the edges are brown, 12 to 15 minutes.

Working quickly, use a thin-edged spatula to lift up one cookie at a time. Flip it over facedown onto a clean work surface. Set a paper fortune in the middle of the cookie and fold the cookie in half, then rest the straight edge of the cookie on the rim of the coffee mug and gently press down to create a fortune cookie shape. Place the still-warm cookie in the muffin tin to cool and keep its shape. You'll have about 10 seconds to shape all the baked cookies before they harden. Repeat to bake and shape the remaining cookies.

/

All fortunes should be viewed through rose-colored glasses, don't you think? These cookies get their lovely pink color from hibiscus flowers and dragon fruit.

BEET-BALLS WITH PICKLED TURNIP DIP

Makes 15 balls and
1 quart (1 L) pickles

Pickled Turnip Dip
1 cup (240 ml) rice vinegar or
   white wine vinegar
1 cup (240 ml) water
2 teaspoons sugar
1 teaspoon fine sea salt
2 strips of grapefruit peel
   (use a vegetable peeler)
1 teaspoon whole pink
   peppercorns
2 bunches Tokyo turnips
   (1 pound/450 g), quartered,
   or large turnips, peeled and
   cut into ¼-inch (6 mm)
   pieces
1 small red beet, peeled and
   quartered
4 dates, pitted and finely
   chopped
½ cup (125 g) plain whole-milk
   yogurt
1 teaspoon ground sumac

Beet-Balls
2 medium red beets (about
   12 ounces/340 g), peeled
½ cup (60 g) walnuts
1 (15-ounce/425 g) can kidney
   beans, drained and rinsed
½ red onion, coarsely chopped
4 red chard leaves (with
   stems), stems finely
   chopped and leaves thinly
   sliced
¼ cup (35 g) dry bread crumbs
2 large eggs
¾ teaspoon pink salt
Freshly ground pink pepper
Extra-virgin olive oil

½ teaspoon Aleppo pepper,
   for garnish

Make the pickled turnips: In a small nonreactive saucepan, combine the vinegar, water, sugar, salt, grapefruit peel, and pink peppercorns. Bring to a boil. Add the turnips and beet and immediately remove the pot from the heat. Let the turnips cool to room temperature in the brine. Transfer the turnips with their brine to a jar, cover, and refrigerate for at least 1 week before serving.

Make the beet-balls: Preheat the oven to 400°F (200°C). Line a baking sheet with parchment paper.

Cut the beets into large pieces and place them in a food processor. Process until finely chopped, then transfer to a large bowl.

In a dry skillet, toast the walnuts over medium heat, stirring often, until golden, 3 to 5 minutes. Transfer them to the food processor (no need to clean it). Add the kidney beans and onion and blend to a thick paste. Transfer the mixture to the bowl with the beets. Stir in the chard, bread crumbs, eggs, pink salt, and lots of pink pepper. Using your hands, mix well, then shape the mixture into 15 balls. Place them on the prepared baking sheet and drizzle with olive oil. Roast until browned, about 30 minutes.

Meanwhile, chop a large handful of the pickled turnips into matchsticks and place them in a medium bowl along with 1 tablespoon of their pickling brine. Add the dates, yogurt, and sumac. Mix well.

Serve the beet-balls together with the pickled turnip dip. Sprinkle with the Aleppo pepper.

/

No spaghetti here. These fuchsia-colored, vegetarian beet-balls go with creamy pickled turnip dip instead. Plan ahead for the turnips to pickle in your refrigerator for at least one week (or just buy a jar).

CHILLED SUMMER BORSCHT

Serves 8 to 10

4 medium beets (about
    1 pound/450 g), scrubbed
    and tops trimmed
3 medium purple potatoes
    (about 12 ounces/340 g),
    scrubbed
Fine sea salt
2 cups (480 ml) good-quality
    chicken broth
2 cups (480 ml) buttermilk
1 cup (225 g) sour cream, plus
    more for serving
3 tablespoons fresh lemon
    juice
1 tablespoon white wine
    vinegar
Freshly ground black pepper
½ large English cucumber,
    peeled and cut into ½-inch
    (1.5 cm) cubes
¼ small red cabbage, cored
    and sliced into very thin
    ribbons
4 scallions, white and green
    parts, thinly sliced
1 small bunch dill, finely
    chopped
Chive blossoms, for garnish

Peel the beets and cut them and the purple potatoes into 1-inch (2.5 cm) pieces. Place the beets in a large pot, fill the pot with cool water, season generously with salt, and bring to a boil. After about 20 minutes, add the potatoes to the pot and continue cooking for another 20 minutes until all the vegetables are tender when pierced with a fork. Use a slotted spoon to transfer the cooked vegetables to a plate.

Strain 2 cups (480 ml) of the cooking liquid through a fine-mesh sieve into a large bowl. Add the chicken broth, buttermilk, sour cream, lemon juice, vinegar, and lots of pepper. Taste and season with more salt if needed.

Add the cooked beets and potatoes to the broth along with the cucumber, cabbage, scallions, and dill. Stir gently. Cover and refrigerate for at least 4 hours before serving. Garnish each bowl of chilled soup with a sprinkling of chive blossoms.

/

Stunningly hot pink. Fresh lemon juice, buttermilk, and white wine vinegar bring some welcome tartness to this chilled soup. Serve it ice-cold on the hottest day of the year.

PURPLE LETTUCES WITH KALAMATA, PLUM, AND VERJUS-GRETTE

Serves 2 to 4

1 head red butter lettuce
1 head Treviso
Handful red shiso leaves
1 small garlic clove, peeled
Fine sea salt
2 tablespoons fresh lemon
   juice
1 teaspoon red wine vinegar
3 tablespoons verjus rouge
Freshly ground black pepper
Dijon mustard
¼ cup (60 ml) extra-virgin
   olive oil
¼ cup (35 g) pitted kalamata
   olives
2 plums, pitted and sliced
4 fresh purple figs, quartered

Separate the butter lettuce and Treviso heads into individual leaves. Trim any green parts from the butter lettuce (and save them for another purpose). Rinse and thoroughly dry the lettuce, Treviso, and shiso leaves.

Using a mortar and pestle or the back of a large knife, pound the garlic and a pinch of salt to a smooth paste. Transfer to a small bowl and stir in the lemon juice, vinegar, verjus, ¼ teaspoon salt, and several grinds of pepper. Dip the tines of a clean fork into the mustard jar. When you lift the fork, a small amount of mustard should cling to the tines. Dunk the fork into the lemon juice mixture and stir to incorporate. Pour in the olive oil and stir until emulsified.

In a large bowl, combine the lettuce, Treviso, and shiso leaves with the olives, plums, and figs. Season with a pinch or two of salt, then add about half the vinaigrette and very gently toss the salad using your hands. Taste a leaf and add more dressing if you like. Serve right away.

/

Purple lettuces like Treviso, red butter lettuce, and red shiso have rich mauve tones, just like kalamata olives. The similarly hued ingredients come together in this salad and are united by a vinaigrette made with verjus rouge, a nonalcoholic grape juice.

PICKLED PURPLE CARROT AND CABBAGE SLAW

Serves 6

1 bunch purple carrots
Juice of ½ lemon
2 tablespoons apple cider
    vinegar
Fine sea salt
1 small red cabbage, cored
¼ cup (60 ml) extra-virgin
    olive oil

Cut the carrots in half lengthwise. Use a vegetable peeler to create long, thin ribbons. Place the carrot ribbons in a large bowl and add the lemon juice, vinegar, and ¼ teaspoon salt. Set aside to pickle at room temperature for about 10 minutes.

Meanwhile, slice the cabbage as thinly as possible into long, wavy ribbons. When the carrots are done pickling, add the cabbage to the bowl and toss to combine. Drizzle in the olive oil and season with a little more salt. Serve.

/

A tangle of pickled purple carrot and red cabbage ribbons comes together to make a slaw like you've never seen before.

BEET RICOTTA GNOCCHI

Serves 6

2 large red beets (about
   1¼ pounds/565 g)
1¼ cups (310 g) fresh whole-
   milk basket ricotta
1 cup (110 g) grated
   Parmigiano-Reggiano
   cheese
1 large egg
4 cups (500 g) all-purpose
   flour, plus more for shaping
Semolina flour, for dusting
Fine sea salt
Extra-virgin olive oil
Pink salt
Freshly ground pink
   peppercorns

Preheat the oven to 400°F (200°C).

Wrap each beet individually in aluminum foil, place them on a baking sheet, and roast until completely tender when poked with a fork, 1 to 2 hours.

Unwrap the beets, discarding the foil, and let cool until you can comfortably handle them. Peel the beets, cut them into large chunks, and place in a food processor. Process to a smooth purée. Transfer the beet purée to a large bowl and add the ricotta, Parmigiano, and egg. Mix until well combined. Add the flour and gently mix it in until just barely incorporated. Cover and let rest at room temperature for 30 minutes.

Line a baking sheet with parchment paper and dust with semolina. On a lightly floured work surface, divide the dough into 4 equal pieces. Working with one piece at a time, roll the dough into a log about ½ inch (1.5 cm) in diameter. Cut the log crosswise into 1-inch (2.5 cm) pieces. Transfer the gnocchi to the prepared baking sheet, making sure they don't touch. Repeat with the remaining dough.

Bring a large pot of generously salted water to a boil. Add the gnocchi and cook until they float, 1 to 3 minutes. Use a slotted spoon to transfer the cooked gnocchi to serving plates or bowls. Drizzle with olive oil and season with pink salt and pink pepper.

/

You might think red beets plus white fresh ricotta would make pink, but as it turns out, the natural acidity from the cheese shifts the color of these gnocchi toward a purple hue.

QUINOA WITH WATERMELON RADISH AND DRIED SOUR CHERRIES

Serves 4 to 6

1½ cups (255 g) uncooked
  red quinoa, rinsed well
3 cups (720 ml) water
½ teaspoon fine sea salt
3 egg-size watermelon
  radishes or purple radishes
  (about 9 ounces/255 g)
½ cup (80 g) dried sour cherries
¼ cup (60 ml) extra-virgin
  olive oil
¼ cup (60 ml) red wine vinegar
1 teaspoon ground sumac

In a small saucepan with a lid, combine the quinoa, water, and salt. Bring to a boil, then adjust the heat so the water simmers gently. Cook, uncovered, until the quinoa has absorbed all the water, about 15 minutes. Remove the pan from the heat, cover with the lid, and let steam for 5 minutes.

Meanwhile, peel the radishes and slice them crosswise as thinly as possible.

Uncover the quinoa and fluff it with a fork. Mix in the dried cherries, olive oil, and vinegar, then gently fold in the sliced radishes. Garnish with the sumac. Serve warm.

/

Red quinoa should be called purple quinoa. Its majestic tone shines in this salad with dark dried sour cherries and watermelon radish.

PURPLE SWEET POTATO PIE BARS WITH CORNMEAL CRUST

Makes 24 bars

Crust
1¼ cups (2½ sticks/280 g) unsalted butter, at room temperature
½ cup packed (105 g) brown sugar
¼ cup (50 g) granulated sugar
2 cups (250 g) all-purpose flour
½ cup (70 g) blue cornmeal
¾ teaspoon fine sea salt

Filling
2 large purple sweet potatoes (about 2 pounds/910 g), scrubbed
1 (12-ounce/355 ml) can evaporated milk
1 cup packed (215 g) brown sugar
3 large eggs
6 tablespoons (¾ stick/85 g) unsalted butter, melted and cooled slightly
1 teaspoon pure vanilla extract
½ teaspoon ube extract
½ teaspoon fine sea salt

Line the bottom of a 9 by 13-inch (23 by 33 cm) pan with parchment paper.

Make the crust: Using a stand mixer fitted with the paddle attachment, beat the butter, brown sugar, and granulated sugar on high speed until light and fluffy, about 4 minutes. Add the flour, cornmeal, and salt. Mix on low speed until just combined. Transfer the very sticky dough to the prepared pan and use a rubber spatula to press it evenly over the bottom. Refrigerate until firm.

Preheat the oven to 350°F (175°C).

Bake the crust until golden brown, about 30 minutes. Let cool while you make the filling; keep the oven on.

Make the filling: Use a fork to prick the sweet potatoes all over. Microwave until tender when poked with the fork, 10 to 15 minutes. Cut the potatoes in half and scoop the flesh into a food processor. (Discard the skins—or crisp them in a hot skillet with plenty of olive oil and eat them as a snack.) Pulse until smooth, then transfer the sweet potato purée to a very large bowl. Add the evaporated milk, brown sugar, eggs, melted butter, vanilla, ube extract, and salt. Whisk until fully incorporated. Pour the filling into the crust. Bake until just set in the middle, about 50 minutes. Let cool completely before cutting into bars and serving.

/

Ready to flip a tradition on its head? These bars are just like pumpkin pie, except they're purple! They're flavored with sweet, vanilla-scented ube, and even their crust has some extra flecks of color thanks to blue cornmeal.

SWEET-AND-SOUR EGGPLANT, SICHUAN-STYLE

Serves 4 to 6

3 large Asian eggplants
    (about 1½ pounds/680 g)
¾ teaspoon fine sea salt
6 tablespoons (90 ml)
    vegetable oil
3 garlic cloves, finely grated
1 (2-inch/5 cm) piece fresh
    ginger, peeled and finely
    grated
1 tablespoon doubanjiang
    (Sichuan chile bean paste)
¾ cup (180 ml) good-quality
    chicken broth
3 tablespoons soy sauce or
    tamari
1 tablespoon sugar
¾ teaspoon cornstarch, mixed
    with 1 tablespoon cold
    water to form a slurry
1 tablespoon black vinegar or
    rice vinegar

Cut the eggplants into batons about 3 inches (7.5 cm) long and ¾ inch (2 cm) thick. Toss them with the salt in a colander and let stand for 30 minutes.

Heat a large nonreactive skillet over medium-high heat for 2 minutes. Swirl in 3 tablespoons of the vegetable oil, then add half the eggplant and cook until browned on one side, about 2 minutes. Flip and sear on the other side until nicely caramelized, 1 to 2 minutes. Transfer the eggplant to a plate and repeat to cook the other half, using the remaining 3 tablespoons of vegetable oil.

Return all the eggplant to the pan and lower the heat to medium-low. Add the garlic, ginger, and chile bean paste. Cook, stirring gently, until the garlic softens, 1 minute. Pour in the broth and soy sauce and adjust the heat so the sauce simmers. Stir in the sugar, cornstarch slurry, and vinegar and simmer until the sauce thickens slightly, 1 to 2 minutes. Serve hot.

/

Asian eggplants have shiny, vibrantly purple skins, like jumbo old-fashioned Christmas tree lights. Use them in this dish that's sweet and sour and a little spicy, thanks to a touch of Sichuan chile bean paste.

UVA UBE SCHIACCIATA

Serves 6 to 8

½ cup (120 ml) lukewarm
    water
1 (¼-ounce/7 g) packet active
    dry yeast (2¼ teaspoons)
¼ cup (50 g) plus
    2 tablespoons sugar,
    plus a pinch
2 cups (250 g) all-purpose flour
¼ cup (60 ml) extra-virgin
    olive oil, plus more for the
    pan
¼ teaspoon ube extract
¼ teaspoon fine sea salt
1 pound (450 g) seedless black
    grapes, stemmed
Flaky salt, for sprinkling

In the bowl of a stand mixer fitted with the dough hook, combine the water, yeast, and pinch of sugar. Let stand until the mixture is foamy, about 5 minutes. Add the flour, olive oil, ube extract, salt, and ¼ cup (50 g) of the sugar. Mix on medium-low speed until the dough is smooth, about 7 minutes. Cover with a clean kitchen towel and let rise at room temperature until doubled in size, about 1 hour.

Generously drizzle olive oil across a rimmed baking sheet. Transfer the dough to the prepared baking sheet and use your palms to smooth it out into an even rectangle approximately 11 by 14 inches (28 by 36 cm). Scatter the grapes, pressing them into the dough, and sprinkle the remaining 2 tablespoons sugar on top. Let the schiacciata rise once more at warm room temperature for 1 hour.

About 15 minutes before the schiacciata is done rising, preheat the oven to 400°F (200°C).

Bake until golden brown around the edges and on the bottom, about 20 minutes. Transfer the schiacciata to a wire rack to cool. Sprinkle with flaky salt, cut into squares, and serve warm or at room temperature.

/

Schiacciata is a sweet focaccia-like bread made during the grape (*uva* in Italian) harvest season. Uva and ube sound alike, which is fun, and they share a similar deep purple color.

BLUEBERRY-CHERRY AMARETTI

Makes about 18 cookies

½ cup (110 g) purple sanding
    sugar
1 cup (20 g) freeze-dried
    blueberries
2 large egg whites
1½ cups (145 g) almond flour
⅔ cup (135 g) granulated sugar
18 Amarena cherries

Preheat the oven to 300°F (150°C). Line a baking sheet with parchment paper. Place the sanding sugar in a small shallow dish.

Place the freeze-dried blueberries in a food processor and process to a fine powder.

In a large bowl using a handheld mixer, whip the egg whites until soft peaks form. Add the almond flour, granulated sugar, and blueberry powder. Use a rubber spatula to fold them in until the batter is homogenous and has the texture of a paste.

With two small spoons, scoop up ½-ounce (20 g) balls and roll them in the sanding sugar. Place them on the prepared baking sheet, spacing them evenly apart, and press each one with your thumb to create a dimple. Place an Amarena cherry in each dimple.

Bake the cookies until light golden brown on the bottoms, about 20 minutes. Let cool on the baking sheet.

/

Glistening like jewels, these Amarena cherry–studded almond cookies are gluten-free and get their appealing color from freeze-dried blueberries.

CAULIFLOWER RICE WITH RED ORACH

Serves 4 to 6

1 head purple cauliflower,
    green leaves removed
¼ cup (55 g) ghee or unsalted
    butter
2 teaspoons brown mustard
    seeds
1 teaspoon cumin seeds
1 teaspoon black sesame seeds
½ teaspoon fennel seeds
Fine sea salt
2 cups lightly packed (about
    2 ounces/57 g) red orach
    leaves, sliced into thin
    ribbons
Juice of 1 lemon

Cut the cauliflower (including the stem and core) into large pieces. Place half the cauliflower pieces in a food processor. Pulse until the cauliflower resembles cooked rice—be careful not to overprocess it, or the texture will get mushy. Transfer the riced cauliflower to a bowl and repeat with the other half.

In a large nonreactive skillet, melt the ghee over medium heat. Add the mustard seeds, cumin, sesame seeds, and fennel. Cook until the seeds begin to pop and sputter in the hot oil, about 1 minute. Mix in the cauliflower rice and ½ teaspoon salt. Cook, stirring, until the cauliflower loses its raw flavor, 2 to 3 minutes. Remove the pan from the heat and stir in the orach. Squeeze the lemon juice over everything—the acidity from the lemon will turn the cauliflower a slightly more vibrant red-purple. You can serve it without stirring in the lemon for a tie-dye effect, or mix it well for uniform color.

/

A magical color transformation happens when you squeeze lemon juice over cooked purple cauliflower—the acidity brings forward the pink tones. This dish looks like it was tie-dyed.

BLUE CORN QUESADILLAS

Makes 6 quesadillas

1 cup (115 g) blue corn masa
    harina
1 cup (125 g) all-purpose flour
½ teaspoon butterfly pea
    flower powder
1 teaspoon baking powder
1 teaspoon fine sea salt
5 tablespoons (65 g) lard
1 cup (240 ml) hot water
Vegetable oil, for the pan
6 ounces (170 g) semi-firm
    cheese, such as Monterey
    Jack, grated

In a medium bowl, stir together the masa harina, flour, butterfly pea flower powder, baking powder, and salt. Mix in the lard, using your fingertips to rub the lard into the flour mixture until there are no pieces larger than a pea. Pour in the hot water, stir until well combined, then knead the dough for 3 to 5 minutes. Divide the dough into 12 equal-size balls. Cover with a clean kitchen towel and let rest at room temperature for 30 minutes.

Using a tortilla press or a rolling pin, flatten each ball to a 4- to 5-inch (10 to 12.5 cm) round.

Heat a cast-iron skillet, lightly coated with vegetable oil, over medium heat for 2 minutes. Place one dough round in the skillet and cook until puffed and golden brown in a few places on the first side, about 1 minute. Flip and cook on the second side for another 1 minute. Wrap the cooked tortilla in a clean kitchen towel to stay soft while you cook the remaining dough.

Lower the heat under the skillet to medium-low. Add a little more vegetable oil to the pan if it looks dry. Place 2 tortillas in a single layer in the skillet. Toast on the first side for 1 minute, then remove from the skillet. Place another 2 tortillas in the skillet and toast for 1 minute, then flip. Scatter about one-third of the cheese over the tortillas, dividing it evenly between them. Top with the toasted tortillas, with the untoasted side facing up. Flip and cook until the cheese melts, 1 to 2 minutes. Repeat to cook the remaining quesadillas. Serve hot.

/

**Dusty denim blue. You might
be tempted to use blue cheese
here, but it won't melt the way
you want it to for quesadillas.
Try a meltable semi-firm
cheese like Monterey Jack.**

BLUEBERRY BRANZINO

Serves 4

6 garlic cloves, thinly sliced
1 lemon, cut into very thin
    slices
2 whole branzino (about
    1 pound/455 g each),
    scaled and gutted
4 tablespoons (60 ml)
    extra-virgin olive oil
Fine sea salt
6 bushy rosemary sprigs, plus
    fresh rosemary blossoms,
    for garnish
1 tablespoon balsamic vinegar
1 pint (340 g) fresh blueberries
Fresh borage blossoms,
    for garnish

Preheat the oven to 425°F (220°C).

In a bowl, toss together the garlic and lemon slices.

Place the fish side by side on a rimmed baking sheet. Brush 2 tablespoons of the olive oil total on both sides of both fish and sprinkle inside and outside with 1 teaspoon salt. Stuff the rosemary sprigs and garlic-lemon inside the fish. Roast until just cooked through and flaky, about 20 minutes.

Meanwhile, in a medium bowl, use a fork to stir together the balsamic vinegar, remaining 2 tablespoons olive oil, and a pinch of salt. Mix in the blueberries.

Divide the blueberry salad among 4 plates. Lift a piece of roasted branzino off the bones and place it—with its iridescent blue skin facing up—on top of the blueberries. Scatter the borage blossoms and rosemary blossoms over the fish and serve.

/

Branzino skin shimmers with a pearly cerulean luminescence. Blueberries might be an unexpected pairing here, but they fit right in and look like a bed of wave-smoothed pebbles.

MARBLED SUGAR COOKIES

Makes about 30 cookies

2 cups (250 g) all-purpose
    flour, plus more for rolling
½ teaspoon baking powder
½ teaspoon fine sea salt
¾ cup (1½ sticks/170 g)
    unsalted butter, at room
    temperature
¾ cup (150 g) sugar
1 large egg
½ teaspoon pure lemon extract
    or almond extract
1 tablespoon butterfly pea
    flower powder

In a medium bowl, whisk together the flour, baking powder, and salt.

In the bowl of a stand mixer fitted with the paddle attachment, beat the butter and sugar on medium-high speed until light and fluffy, about 4 minutes. Mix in the egg and lemon extract. Add the flour mixture and mix on low speed until just combined.

Scoop out half the dough, wrap it in plastic wrap, and refrigerate for 1 hour.

Add the butterfly pea flower powder to the remaining dough and mix until evenly incorporated. Wrap the blue dough in plastic wrap and refrigerate for 1 hour.

Preheat the oven to 325°F (165°C). Line two baking sheets with parchment paper.

On a lightly floured surface, divide the white dough and the blue dough into 3 equal pieces each. Arrange them in a rectangle, alternating colors, then smash them all together and knead two or three times to create a marbled pattern. Roll out the dough to just under ¼ inch (6 mm) thick. Cut out shapes using a lightly floured cookie cutter. Place the cookies on the prepared baking sheets, spacing them at least 1 inch (2.5 cm) apart. Bake, rotating the sheets halfway through, until the edges of the cookies are lightly golden, about 12 minutes. Let cool for about 5 minutes on the baking sheets, then transfer to a wire rack to cool completely.

/

These cookies are like the colors of a blue-veined marble slab but inverted. Best to stick to clear lemon or almond extract, which, unlike vanilla, won't impart any brown color.

PRESSED FLOWER SHORTBREAD

Makes about 20 cookies

¾ cup (1½ sticks/170 g)
   unsalted butter, at room
   temperature
¾ cup (150 g) sugar
½ teaspoon fine sea salt
1 large egg yolk
1 teaspoon pure vanilla extract
2 cups (250 g) all-purpose
   flour, plus more for dusting
Fresh or dried edible blue
   flowers (such as cornflower/
   bachelor's button, borage,
   viola, and pansy)

In the bowl of a stand mixer fitted with the paddle attachment, beat the butter and sugar on medium-high speed until light and fluffy, about 4 minutes. Mix in the salt, egg yolk, and vanilla. Add the flour and mix on low speed until just combined.

Place the dough between two large sheets of parchment paper. Roll it out to just under ½ inch (1.5 cm) thick. Use a lightly floured round cookie cutter to stamp out cookies, then decorate them with the flowers. (If the flowers are fresh, simply place them on top of the dough. If they are dried, soak them in warm water for a few minutes, pat completely dry, and place on the dough.) Cover with the parchment again and gently roll to press the flowers into the dough. Transfer the cookies to the prepared baking sheet. Repeat with the dough scraps to make as many cookies as you can. Cover with plastic wrap and freeze for at least 8 hours or up to 3 days.

When you're ready to bake the cookies, preheat the oven to 350°F (175°C). Line a baking sheet with parchment paper.

Space out the cookies on the prepared baking sheet, leaving at least ½ inch (1.5 cm) between them. Bake, rotating the pan halfway through, until the edges of the cookies are golden, about 15 minutes. Transfer to a wire rack to cool.

/

There's a wide variety of edible blue flowers, from the periwinkle hue of borage blossoms to the deeper cobalt of bachelor's buttons. Try to use a combination of blooms for these cookies.

BUTTERFLY PEA FLOWER ICE CREAM

**Makes about 1 quart (1 L)
ice cream**

2 cups (480 ml) heavy cream
1 cup (240 ml) whole milk
⅔ cup (135 g) sugar
**¼ cup (5 g) dried butterfly pea
flowers**
Pinch of fine sea salt
6 large egg yolks

In a medium saucepan, combine the cream, milk, sugar, butterfly pea flowers, and salt. Warm over medium heat, whisking occasionally, until the sugar dissolves and the mixture is barely simmering.

In a medium bowl, whisk the egg yolks to break them up. While whisking continuously, slowly stream in about ¼ cup (60 ml) of the hot cream mixture and whisk to incorporate. Pour the tempered egg yolk mixture into the pot with the remaining hot cream mixture and cook over medium-low heat, stirring continuously with a wooden spoon or rubber spatula, until the cream thickens enough to coat the back of the spoon and registers 170°F (77°C) on an instant-read thermometer, about 5 minutes.

Strain the custard through a fine-mesh sieve into a large bowl. Cover with a piece of plastic wrap pressed directly against the surface of the custard and refrigerate for at least 4 hours and up to 3 days.

Transfer the chilled custard to an ice cream maker and churn according to the manufacturer's instructions. Before serving, let the ice cream warm up for a few minutes at room temperature until scoopable.

/

**This is the color of the sky
above San Francisco when the
summer fog burns off midday.**

BLUE OYSTER MUSHROOM BAO

Makes 12 buns

¾ cup (180 ml) warm water
1½ tablespoons sugar
1 (¼-ounce/7 g) packet active
    dry yeast (2¼ teaspoons)
2½ cups (315 g) all-purpose
    flour, plus more for dusting
1 tablespoon butterfly pea
    flower powder
2 teaspoons baking powder
3 tablespoons vegetable oil
3 tablespoons sesame oil
1 (2-inch/5 cm) piece fresh
    ginger, peeled and finely
    grated
4 garlic cloves, finely grated or
    minced
About 12 ounces (350 g) blue
    oyster mushrooms, finely
    chopped (about 4 cups)
2 tablespoons soy sauce or
    tamari
1 tablespoon rice vinegar
2 teaspoons doubanjiang
    (Sichuan chile bean paste)
2 teaspoons cornstarch
2 tablespoons water

/

Puffy steamed bao aren't traditionally blue—apologies to the purists—but these are stuffed with blue oyster mushrooms, and it only seemed appropriate to match the dough to the filling.

In the bowl of a stand mixer fitted with the dough hook, stir together the warm water, sugar, and yeast. Let stand until the mixture is foamy, about 5 minutes.

Add the flour, butterfly pea flower powder, baking powder, and vegetable oil. Mix on medium speed until the dough comes together, then knead until smooth, 5 to 7 minutes. Cover the bowl and place in a warm spot to rise until doubled in size, about 1 hour.

Meanwhile, in a large sauté pan, warm 1 tablespoon of the sesame oil over medium-high heat. Add the ginger and garlic and cook, stirring continuously, for 1 minute. Add the mushrooms and the remaining 2 tablespoons sesame oil and cook, stirring occasionally, until tender and browned in a few places, 6 to 8 minutes. Mix in the soy sauce, vinegar, and chile bean paste. In a small bowl, stir together the cornstarch and water, then pour this slurry into the pan, stir well, and let bubble for 1 minute. Remove from the heat and let cool.

Cut twelve 3-inch (7.5 cm) square sheets of parchment and arrange them in two bamboo steamer baskets.

On a lightly floured surface, divide the dough into 12 equal pieces. Roll each piece into a ball, then flatten it into a round about 4 inches (10 cm) in diameter. Spoon about 1 tablespoon of the filling into the middle of the dough round, then gather up the edges around the filling and pinch them together at the top to enclose the filling and create a bun shaped like a coin purse. Place the shaped bun on one of the parchment squares. Repeat with the remaining dough and filling. Cover the baskets and let rise in a warm spot until puffy but not quite doubled in size, 30 minutes or so.

Stack the steamer baskets over a pan of simmering water and cover with the steamer lid. Steam the buns until fluffy and cooked through, about 10 minutes.

BLUE JEAN EASTER EGG BREADS

Makes 4 breads

4 cups (360 g) chopped red
    cabbage (from ½ small
    cabbage)

4 cups (960 ml) plus 1 teaspoon
    water

2 tablespoons white vinegar

7 large white eggs

1 cup (240 ml) whole milk

1 (¼-ounce/7 g) packet active
    dry yeast (2¼ teaspoons)

3 tablespoons sugar

4 to 4½ cups (500 to 560 g)
    all-purpose flour

1 teaspoon spirulina powder

2 teaspoons fine sea salt

4 tablespoons (½ stick/57 g)
    unsalted butter, at room
    temperature, plus more for
    greasing

/

Who needs a chemical dye
when you can use red cabbage
to give Easter eggs the same
exact color as broken-in blue
jeans?

In a nonreactive medium saucepan, combine the cabbage and
4 cups (960 ml) of the water. Bring to a gentle simmer. Cook, stirring
occasionally, until the water is deeply colored, about 30 minutes.
Let cool completely.

Strain the liquid through a fine-mesh sieve and discard the cabbage.
Stir in the vinegar, then gently add 4 of the eggs. Refrigerate for
4 hours (for light blue eggs), overnight (for deep ocean blue eggs),
or for up to 2 days if you'd like the blue color to be even darker.

Warm the milk to body temperature, then pour it into the bowl of a
stand mixer or a large bowl. Sprinkle the yeast and 1 tablespoon of
the sugar over the milk and stir until dissolved. Set aside for about
5 minutes, until bubbling and lightly foamy.

Add the remaining 2 tablespoons sugar, 4 cups (500 g) of the flour,
the spirulina, salt, and 2 of the undyed eggs. Using the dough hook
of the stand mixer or a large spoon, mix until a stiff dough forms.
While mixing, add little pieces of the butter, a few at a time, until
all the butter has been incorporated. Mix on low speed or knead on
an unfloured surface for about 10 minutes. The dough should be just
sticky enough to stick to the bottom but not the sides of the bowl.
If the dough is very sticky, add up to ½ cup (65 g) additional flour
1 tablespoon at a time. Place the dough in a greased bowl, cover with
a clean kitchen towel, and let rise in a warm spot for 90 minutes.

Line a baking sheet with parchment paper. Divide the dough into
8 equal pieces. Using your palms, roll each piece into a 16-inch-long
(41 cm) rope. Working with two pieces at a time, pinch the ends
together and twist the ropes around themselves. Coil the twist into
a loose circle with a 1-inch (2.5 cm) hole in the center. Set the loop
of dough on the prepared baking sheet. Repeat with the remaining
ropes to make 4 loops of dough total. Place 1 dyed egg in the middle
of each loop, pressing gently so that it's snug. Cover with the kitchen
towel and let rise in a warm spot for 1 hour.

About 15 minutes before the end of the rising time, preheat the oven
to 375°F (190°C).

Beat together the remaining undyed egg and remaining 1 teaspoon
water to make an egg wash. Brush the egg wash over the dough.
Bake until the breads are shiny and deep golden brown along the
ridges, about 20 minutes. Let cool slightly before serving.

OMBRÉ CRÊPE CAKE

Makes one 8-inch (20 cm) cake

2 cups (250 g) all-purpose flour
¼ cup (50 g) granulated sugar
½ teaspoon fine sea salt
4 large eggs
1½ teaspoons pure almond
  extract
4 tablespoons (½ stick/57 g)
  unsalted butter, melted,
  plus more at room
  temperature for the pan
1½ cups (360 ml) whole milk
½ cup (120 ml) light-colored
  beer
1¾ teaspoons butterfly pea
  flower powder
Scant 1 teaspoon spirulina
  powder
1 cup (240 ml) heavy cream
1 cup (240 g) crème fraîche
¾ cup (95 g) confectioners'
  sugar

In a large bowl, combine the flour, granulated sugar, and salt. Whisk in the eggs, almond extract, melted butter, milk, and beer. Cover and refrigerate overnight.

Divide the batter evenly among eight small bowls or cups. Stir 1 teaspoon of the butterfly pea flower powder into one bowl, ½ teaspoon into the second bowl, and ¼ teaspoon into the third bowl. Stir ½ teaspoon spirulina into the fourth bowl, ¼ teaspoon into the fifth, ⅛ teaspoon into the sixth, and ₁/₁₆ teaspoon into the seventh. Leave the eighth bowl white.

Heat an 8-inch (20 cm) nonstick pan over medium heat. Swirl in a little butter. While tilting the pan, pour in half of the batter from the white bowl. Cook just until the edges brown and look dry, 30 seconds to 1 minute. Flip and cook on the other side for about 10 seconds. Transfer the crêpe to a plate. Repeat to cook the remaining white batter and stack the crêpe on the plate. Continue cooking the crêpes, two per bowl of batter, starting with the lightest blue batter and finishing with the darkest blue batter. Add butter to the pan as needed between crêpes.

To assemble the cake, whip the cream until it holds perky peaks in a medium bowl. Stir in the crème fraîche and confectioners' sugar. Place one white crêpe on a serving plate. Spread a thin layer of sweetened crème fraîche over the crêpe, then top with the other white crêpe. Continue layering, creating an ombré pattern from lightest to darkest blue crêpes. Serve right away or refrigerate until ready to serve.

/

The ombré effect of this cake is like diving deeper into the blue of the sea. It's a real showstopper!

BLUE MADELEINES

Makes about 24 madeleines

1 cup (125 g) all-purpose flour,
    plus more for dusting
1 tablespoon butterfly pea
    flower powder
¾ teaspoon baking powder
¼ teaspoon fine sea salt
3 large eggs
¾ cup (150 g) sugar
½ cup (1 stick/115 g) unsalted
    butter, melted and cooled
    slightly, plus more at room
    temperature for the pans

In a small bowl, whisk together the flour, butterfly pea flower powder, baking powder, and salt.

In a large bowl using a handheld mixer, beat the eggs and sugar on high speed until thick and pale, 6 to 7 minutes. Sift in the flour mixture and fold gently to incorporate. Fold in the melted butter. Cover the batter and refrigerate for at least 2 hours and up to 3 days.

Preheat the oven to 375°F (190°C). Generously butter and flour two 12-well madeleine pans.

Scoop 1 tablespoon of the batter into each well of the prepared pans. Bake the madeleines until the edges are golden brown and the center springs back when lightly pressed, 8 to 10 minutes. Remove the madeleines from the pan by tapping the pan on the counter. Serve right away.

/

When these little cake-cookies bake, their tops stay turquoise in color while their bottoms turn golden. They end up looking like seashells that were tossed around on a sandy beach.

SKY DUMPLINGS

Makes 16 dumplings

2½ cups (315 g) all-purpose
    flour
½ teaspoon spirulina powder
¼ teaspoon fine sea salt
⅔ cup (160 ml) boiling water
¾ pound (340 g) ground pork
2 cups (180 g) shredded Napa
    cabbage
1 bunch chives, chopped
1 (2-inch/5 cm) piece fresh
    ginger, peeled and finely
    grated
2 tablespoons soy sauce or
    tamari, plus more for
    serving
2 teaspoons toasted sesame oil
Black vinegar or rice vinegar,
    for serving

In a large bowl, whisk together the flour, spirulina, and salt. Pour in the boiling water and stir to incorporate. Transfer the dough to a clean work surface and knead it until smooth, about 5 minutes. If the dough feels stiff, wet your hands with hot tap water and continue kneading. Repeat as necessary. Cover with a clean kitchen towel and let rest at room temperature for 30 minutes.

Meanwhile, in the same large bowl (it doesn't need to be cleaned), combine the pork, cabbage, chives, ginger, soy sauce, and sesame oil. Mix well.

Fill a small bowl with water and set it nearby.

Divide the dough into 2 equal pieces. Working with one piece at a time and keeping the other piece covered, roll the dough into a rope approximately 16 inches (40 cm) long. Cut the rope into 16 equal pieces. Roll each piece to a flat circle, about 4 inches (10 cm) in diameter. Repeat with the other half of the dough.

Place one dough round in the palm of your nondominant hand. Spoon a rounded ½ tablespoon of filling into the center of the dough round. Dip your finger in the water and use it to moisten the edge of the wrapper. Fold the wrapper in half, around the filling, and pinch the edges closed to seal. Make three pleats on the right side of the curved edge of the dumpling, pinching each pleat firmly to seal, then make three pleats on the left side of the curved edge. The pleats should all point toward the center to give the dumpling a crescent shape. Repeat to form the remaining dumplings.

To cook the dumplings, bring a pot of water to a simmer. Add as many dumplings as will fit comfortably in the pot and cook for about 5 minutes. Repeat to boil the other dumplings in batches. Serve steaming hot, with soy sauce and vinegar if you like.

/

Spirulina, a blue-green algae, gives these dumplings their surprising oceanic shade.

MERMAID BOWLS

Serves 2 to 4

½ cup (120 ml) oat milk or cow milk
6 tablespoons (95 g) plain whole-milk yogurt, plus more for garnish
2 bananas, peeled and frozen
1 tart apple (such as Granny Smith), peeled, cored, and chopped
2 teaspoons spirulina powder
2 cups (480 ml) ice cubes
½ cup (85 g) frozen blueberries
½ cup (70 g) frozen blackberries
2 kiwifruits, peeled and cut into star-shaped slices
1 white-fleshed dragon fruit

In a blender, combine the milk, yogurt, bananas, apple, spirulina, and ice cubes. Blend on high speed until completely smooth. Spoon into small serving bowls. Swirl a spoonful of yogurt into each bowl to garnish, creating a barreling wave pattern, then top with the frozen berries and kiwi. Use a melon baller to scoop balls of dragon fruit and add them to the bowls.

/

This spirulina smoothie bowl is topped with aquamarine-colored fruits. Frosty blueberries and blackberries have a scaly glisten to them, while pops of kiwi make this dish appear as teal as a mermaid's tail.

APPLE-FENNEL SALAD WITH GOAT CHEESE AND PISTACHIO PESTO

Serves 4 to 6

Pistachio Pesto
1¼ cups (25 g) fresh basil leaves
⅓ cup (45 g) shelled pistachios, toasted
1 garlic clove, peeled
Finely grated zest from 1 lime
1 tablespoon fresh lime juice
Fine sea salt
⅓ cup (80 ml) extra-virgin olive oil

Salad
1 small garlic clove, peeled
Fine sea salt
3 tablespoons fresh lemon juice
¼ cup (60 ml) extra-virgin olive oil
2 tart green apples (such as Pippin or Granny Smith)
1 fennel bulb, leafy fronds trimmed
Leaves from 1 bunch dill, finely chopped
4 ounces (115 g) fresh goat cheese
Flaky sea salt
Freshly ground green peppercorns

Make the pesto: In a food processor, combine the basil, pistachios, garlic, lime zest, lime juice, and ½ teaspoon fine salt and process until finely chopped. Pour in the olive oil and process until mostly smooth. Taste and season with more salt.

Make the salad: Using a mortar and pestle or the side of a knife, crush the garlic and a pinch of fine salt to a paste. Transfer the garlic paste to a small bowl (or keep it in the mortar) and stir in the lemon juice. Let stand until the garlic mellows, about 5 minutes, then whisk in the olive oil.

Core and thinly slice the apples. Place them in a large bowl, immediately drizzle with the dressing, and toss to coat.

Slice the fennel as thinly as possible. Add the sliced fennel and dill to the bowl with the apples and toss to incorporate.

Spread about half of the pistachio pesto over a serving platter. Pile the apple-fennel mixture on top. Use your fingers to break the goat cheese into bite-size crumbles, scatter them over the top, and toss very gently one last time. Season the salad with a pinch or two of flaky salt, use a spoon to dollop the remaining pistachio pesto on top, and finish with a few grinds of green pepper.

/

Pale green tart apples and thinly sliced fennel are flecked with chopped dill and tossed with verdant pistachio pesto. The finished dish looks like a mosaic.

MATCHA AND MINT
ICE CREAM SUNDAE

Makes 1 quart (1 L) matcha ice cream and 1 quart (1 L) mint ice cream

Mint Ice Cream
2 cups (60 g) fresh spinach leaves
¼ cup (60 ml) water
1 bunch mint
2 cups (480 ml) heavy cream
1 cup (240 ml) whole milk
⅔ cup (135 g) sugar
Pinch of fine sea salt
2 large egg yolks

Matcha Ice Cream
2 cups (480 ml) heavy cream
1 cup (240 ml) whole milk
⅔ cup (135 g) sugar
Pinch of fine sea salt
2 large egg yolks
3 tablespoons matcha

Fresh mint leaves, for garnish
Matcha, for garnish

/

Two different shades of green, both with lots of white mixed into them from milk and cream.

Make the mint ice cream: Use a blender to purée the spinach and water. Strain through a fine-mesh sieve and set aside.

In a medium heavy-bottomed saucepan, combine the mint, cream, milk, sugar, and salt. Warm the mixture over medium heat, whisking occasionally, until the sugar dissolves and the mixture is steaming-hot but not yet boiling. Remove from the heat, cover, and let steep for 10 minutes, then remove and discard the mint.

In a medium bowl, whisk the egg yolks to break them up. While whisking continuously, slowly stream in about ¼ cup (60 ml) of the hot cream mixture and whisk until incorporated. Pour the tempered egg yolk mixture into the pot with the remaining hot cream and cook over low heat, stirring continuously with a wooden spoon or rubber spatula, until the custard thickens very slightly and registers 170°F (77°C) on an instant-read thermometer, about 5 minutes.

Strain the custard through a fine-mesh sieve into a large bowl. Stir in 3 tablespoons of the spinach water. Cover with a piece of plastic wrap pressed directly against the surface of the custard to prevent a skin from forming and refrigerate for at least 4 hours or up to 3 days.

Pour the chilled custard into an ice cream maker and churn according to the manufacturer's instructions.

Serve right away, or pack the ice cream into a freezer-safe container, press a piece of parchment paper directly against the surface of the ice cream, cover tightly with the lid, and store in the back of the freezer until ready to serve.

Make the matcha ice cream: Follow the same steps as for the mint ice cream, but leave out the spinach, water, and mint. Stir in the matcha after you've strained the custard.

To serve, make a sundae with a scoop of matcha ice cream and a scoop of mint ice cream. Garnish with a fresh mint leaf and a sprinkle of matcha.

LITTLE GEM CAESAR WITH SPINACH CROUTONS

Serves 4 to 6

Dressing
3 small garlic cloves, peeled
4 anchovies, rinsed
Fine sea salt
½ bunch flat-leaf parsley
1 large egg yolk
¾ cup (180 ml) extra-virgin
   olive oil
Juice of ½ lemon
1 tablespoon red wine vinegar
¼ cup (30 g) grated
   Parmigiano-Reggiano cheese
Freshly ground green
   peppercorns

Croutons
4 cups (120 g) fresh spinach
   leaves
3 garlic cloves, peeled
½ cup (1 stick/115 g)
   unsalted butter, at room
   temperature
½ cup (55 g) grated
   Parmigiano-Reggiano
   cheese
1 loaf soft Italian-style bread

4 large heads Little Gem
   lettuce
Freshly ground green
   peppercorns

/

Chartreuse leaves, emerald
dressing, and fern croutons.

Make the dressing: Using a mortar and pestle, pound the garlic, anchovies, and 2 or 3 pinches of salt into a paste. Transfer the paste to a food processor, add the parsley, and process until very finely chopped.

Place the egg yolk in a medium bowl and whisk to break it up. While whisking continuously, add the olive oil drop by drop until the mixture thickens, looks sticky, and pulls away from the sides of the bowl. Continue whisking and adding more oil, now in a thin, slow stream. Once you've added somewhere between one-third and half the total oil, squeeze in a little lemon juice. While whisking continuously, add the remaining oil, still in a thin, slow stream. The mixture should be as thick as mayonnaise. Stir in the parsley paste, vinegar, Parmigiano, lots of green pepper, and any remaining lemon juice.

Make the croutons: Preheat the oven to 400°F (200°C). Line a baking sheet with parchment paper.

In a food processor, combine the spinach, garlic, butter, and Parmigiano. Purée until smooth.

Cut the crust off the bread, then cut the bread into ¾-inch (2 cm) cubes and place them on the prepared baking sheet. Spread the spinach butter on the bread cubes and use your hands to toss until all the cubes are coated. Bake until crisp, about 20 minutes, stirring halfway through.

In a very large bowl, toss the Little Gems with half the dressing and all the croutons. Taste and add more dressing, if you like. Spread a spoonful of any remaining dressing in an arc on each plate. Garnish each serving of salad with green pepper and eat right away.

KALE RISOTTO

Serves 4 to 6

4 garlic cloves, thinly sliced
¼ cup (60 ml) plus
    3 tablespoons extra-virgin
    olive oil
Fine sea salt
1 large bunch lacinato kale,
    leaves stemmed
1 yellow onion, finely chopped
1½ cups (300 g) uncooked
    risotto rice (such as Arborio
    or Carnaroli)
½ cup (120 ml) white wine
3 to 4 cups (720 to 960 ml)
    good-quality chicken broth
    or water
4 tablespoons (½ stick/57 g)
    unsalted butter
½ cup (55 g) grated
    Parmigiano-Reggiano cheese
½ cup (60 g) roasted salted
    pepitas (pumpkin seeds)

In a Dutch oven or nonreactive wide, deep skillet, cook the garlic in ¼ cup (60 ml) of the olive oil over medium heat until golden, 1 to 2 minutes. Pour the garlic and oil into a blender and let cool.

Bring a large pot of generously salted water to a boil. Add the kale leaves and cook, stirring once or twice, until tender, about 5 minutes. Use tongs to transfer the cooked kale, dripping wet, to the blender. Blend to a smooth purée.

Heat the remaining 3 tablespoons olive oil over medium-high heat in the same pan you used to cook the garlic. Add the onion and a few pinches of salt. Cook, stirring often, until softened, about 5 minutes. Stir in the rice and cook until toasted, 2 minutes. Pour in the wine. Cook, stirring, until most of the liquid has evaporated, about 2 minutes.

Pour in 1½ cups (360 ml) of the broth, adjust the heat so the mixture simmers, and cook, stirring occasionally, until most of the liquid has evaporated again and the rice is starting to stick to the pot, 5 to 10 minutes. Add another 1½ cups (360 ml) of the broth and cook, stirring, until the rice tastes tender, about 5 minutes. If the rice isn't yet tender and there's very little liquid in the pot, pour in the remaining 1 cup (240 ml) broth and cook until the rice is tender.

Remove the pot from the heat and stir in the butter, cheese, and kale purée. Taste and season with more salt if needed. Let rest for 5 minutes or so—it'll thicken a little bit. Serve right away, garnishing each bowl of risotto with a sprinkling of the pepitas.

/

Like freshly mowed midwestern grass. A vibrant shade that evokes summer.

MATCHA-LIME TEACAKE WITH CANDIED MINT

Serves 8

Candied Mint
1 bunch mint
1 or 2 egg whites
Pinch of fine sea salt
Sugar

Teacake
Unsalted butter, for the pan
1½ cups (190 g) all-purpose
   flour, plus more for the pan
2 teaspoons baking powder
¾ teaspoon fine sea salt
2 tablespoons plus ½ teaspoon
   matcha
1 cup (200 g) sugar
3 limes
¾ cup (215 g) plain whole-milk
   Greek yogurt
2 large eggs
½ cup (120 ml) neutral-
   flavored oil, such as
   grapeseed or safflower
Mounded ½ cup (100 g) white
   chocolate chips
2 tablespoons heavy cream

/

Matcha, lime, and mint are
three green ingredients whose
flavors harmonize. The candied
mint leaves on top of this
teacake look spectacular and
complicated but are simple
to make.

Make the candied mint: Snip the mint leaves from the stems and pat the leaves thoroughly dry. In a small bowl, whisk 1 egg white and the salt until foamy. Working with 1 mint leaf at a time, use a soft-bristled brush to paint both sides of the leaf with egg white. Sprinkle a thin layer of sugar evenly over both sides of the leaf. Place the leaf on a wire rack and repeat with the remaining leaves, spacing them out on the rack so they don't overlap. Let the candied mint leaves dry at room temperature overnight, or until crisp.

Make the teacake: Preheat the oven to 350°F (175°C). Generously butter and flour an 8½ by 4½-inch (21 by 11 cm/1.5 L) loaf pan.

In a medium bowl, whisk together the flour, baking powder, salt, and 2 tablespoons of the matcha. Measure the sugar into a large bowl. Use a rasp grater to zest the limes directly into the bowl of sugar. Using your fingertips, pinch and rub the zest into the sugar until the sugar is pale green and fragrant. Add the yogurt and eggs. Whisk vigorously until smooth. Add the flour mixture and whisk until there are no visible streaks of flour. Use a rubber spatula to fold in the oil. Scrape the batter into the prepared pan and smooth the top. Bake until the center of the loaf springs back when lightly pressed, about 1 hour.

Let the cake cool in the pan for about 10 minutes before turning it out onto a wire rack and setting it right-side up to cool completely.

Meanwhile, place the white chocolate chips in a small bowl. Place the cream in a separate microwave-safe small bowl and warm it in the microwave for about 30 seconds, until you see bubbles around the edge of the bowl. Immediately pour the hot cream over the white chocolate. Add the remaining ½ teaspoon matcha and let stand for about 5 minutes until the white chocolate melts, then whisk until the mixture is completely smooth. The matcha ganache will firm up slightly as it cools—when it is thick but pourable, spoon it over the top of the cooled teacake, letting some drip down the sides. Decorate the cake with the candied mint leaves before the ganache fully sets.

LEMONGRASS-CILANTRO TOFU BÁNH MÌ

Serves 4

3 lemongrass stalks

4 garlic cloves, peeled

4 scallions, coarsely chopped

1 (2-inch/5 cm) piece fresh ginger, peeled and finely grated

1 small serrano chile, seeded and coarsely chopped

Finely grated zest and juice of 2 limes

¾ teaspoon fine sea salt

2 bunches cilantro, lower stems trimmed

1 (13.5-ounce/400 ml) can full-fat coconut milk

1 (14-ounce/400 g) package extra-firm tofu, cut into ½-inch-thick (1.5 cm) slabs

4 Vietnamese-style soft baguette rolls

2 Persian cucumbers, thinly sliced lengthwise

1 jalapeño, stemmed and thinly sliced

2 avocados, pitted, peeled, and sliced

Trim off and discard all but the bottom few inches of the lemongrass stalks. Peel away the fibrous green layers until you reach the softer purple-white interior. Chop coarsely and place in a food processor. Add the garlic, scallions, ginger, serrano, lime zest, lime juice, salt, and 1 bunch of cilantro. Process into a paste.

Heat a saucepan over medium-high heat. Open the can of coconut milk and spoon the thick, creamy part that has risen to the top into the pan. Add the lemongrass paste and cook, stirring often, for a few minutes. Pour in the remaining coconut milk and bring to a simmer, then remove from the heat.

Place the tofu in a dish large enough to accommodate the slabs in a single layer. Pour in the lemongrass sauce. Let marinate at room temperature for at least 10 minutes or cover and refrigerate for up to 3 days.

To serve, split the rolls lengthwise, leaving them hinged on one side. Toast them under the broiler for a few minutes, if you like. Meanwhile, coarsely chop the remaining cilantro. Spread some of the lemongrass marinade on the bread. Arrange some lemongrass tofu on one side and top with the cucumber, jalapeño, avocado, and remaining cilantro.

/

A vegan and very green version of bánh mì. The tofu marinates in coconut milk dyed green by cilantro and serrano chile, and then the leftover marinade is spread on the sandwich bread as if it were mayonnaise.

178

ZHOUG-MARINATED FETA AND FAVA TOASTS

Serves 4 to 6

4 garlic cloves, peeled
2 bunches cilantro, lower
stems trimmed
Leaves from 1 bunch flat-leaf
parsley
1 jalapeño, stemmed and cut
into 3 pieces
1 tablespoon sherry vinegar
½ teaspoon cumin seeds
¼ teaspoon ground coriander
¼ teaspoon ground cardamom
Fine sea salt
½ cup (120 ml) extra-virgin
olive oil, plus more for
brushing
6 ounces (170 g) feta cheese
2 pounds (910 g) fava beans in
the pod
Leaves from 4 sprigs mint,
thinly sliced
Finely grated zest and juice of
1 lemon
1 baguette, thinly sliced on
a diagonal
2 tablespoons za'atar

/

A collection of delicious green
ingredients layered together
on toast: springy fava beans,
za'atar, fresh mint leaves,
and the spicy, boldly flavored
Yemeni sauce called zhoug.

Use a food processor to finely chop the garlic. Add the cilantro, parsley, jalapeño, vinegar, cumin, coriander, cardamom, and 1 teaspoon salt. Process until combined. While the machine is running, drizzle in the olive oil in a slow, thin stream. Process until the oil is completely incorporated and the zhoug is bright green and emulsified.

Place the feta in a container large enough for it to fit snugly in a single layer. Spoon the zhoug over the feta so the cheese is completely submerged. Refrigerate for at least 1 hour or up to 3 days before serving.

Bring a pot of water to a boil. Fill a large bowl with ice and water.

Shuck the fava beans from their pods. Drop the shucked beans into the boiling water and cook for 2 to 3 minutes, then drain and plunge them into the ice bath to cool.

When the favas are cool, drain them in a colander and use your fingernail to pierce the outer shell of each bean. Squeeze the beans from their shells into a small bowl or a mortar. Add half the mint, the lemon zest, lemon juice, and ¼ teaspoon salt and mash with a fork or the pestle into a chunky spread. Mix in the remaining whole fava beans. Taste and season with more salt if needed.

Preheat the broiler.

Arrange the baguette slices in a single layer on a baking sheet. Brush them with olive oil and place under the broiler to toast until light golden brown and crisp. Spread each slice with some of the zhoug, spoon some fava bean mash on top, and finish with a few big crumbles of the marinated feta. Sprinkle the za'atar over any exposed white feta, turning it green, and garnish with the remaining mint before serving.

FRENCH LENTILS, BROCCOLINI, AND ARUGULA WITH ITALIAN SALSA VERDE

Serves 6

1½ cups (290 g) dried French green lentils

1 yellow onion, peeled and cut in half

Fine sea salt

2 bunches Broccolini (about 1 pound/450 g)

2 bunches flat-leaf parsley, lower stems trimmed

3 garlic cloves, peeled

2 tablespoons brine-packed capers, drained

3 anchovies

1 hard-boiled egg

Finely grated zest and juice of 1 lemon

½ cup (120 ml) extra-virgin olive oil

4 cups (80 g) arugula

¾ cup (100 g) pitted Castelvetrano olives, chopped

In a medium saucepan, combine the lentils, onion, a few pinches of salt, and about 6 cups (1.4 L) water. Bring to a simmer and cook until the lentils are tender but still hold their shape, 20 to 25 minutes.

Bring another pot of salted water to a boil. Cut off and discard the bottom 2 inches (5 cm) or so of the Broccolini stems. If any stems are thicker than a pencil, cut them in half lengthwise. Add the Broccolini to the boiling water and cook until vibrant green and tender, about 5 minutes. Drain.

In a food processor, combine the parsley, garlic, capers, anchovies, egg, lemon zest, and lemon juice. Process until smooth. While the machine is running, drizzle in the olive oil in a slow, thin stream and process until the oil is completely incorporated and the sauce is bright green and emulsified.

When the lentils are done, drain them and discard the onion. Transfer the cooked lentils and Broccolini to a serving platter. Add the arugula, olives, and salsa verde and toss gently until the lentils, Broccolini, and greens are evenly coated. Serve warm or at room temperature.

/

A hearty green lentil and Broccolini salad. The dressing is a little unusual in that it has one whole hard-boiled egg blended into the mix, which adds some heft and creaminess to balance the abundant bright, fresh herby flavors.

BLISTERED BEANS AND YUZU KOSHO SCALLOPS

Serves 4 to 6

⅓ cup (80 ml) extra-virgin
   olive oil
12 ounces (340 g) green beans,
   ends trimmed
½ teaspoon fine sea salt
6 ounces (170 g) sugar snap
   peas, trimmed and strings
   removed
6 scallions, white and green
   parts, thinly sliced
2 tablespoons unsalted butter
1 pound (450 g) bay or sea
   scallops, patted completely
   dry
1 tablespoon furikake (a very
   green one!)
3 tablespoons yuzu juice
1 tablespoon green yuzu kosho
1 cup (20 g) fresh pea shoots

Heat about half the olive oil in a large stainless-steel skillet over medium-high heat for 1 minute. Add the green beans and ¼ teaspoon of the salt and cook, stirring a few times, until tender and vibrantly green, about 5 minutes. Transfer the cooked green beans to a serving platter, leaving the oil in the pan. Add the remaining oil, sugar snap peas, and the remaining ¼ teaspoon salt. Cook, stirring often, until tender and vibrantly green, about 3 minutes. Add the scallions to the pan and cook, stirring constantly, for 1 minute. Transfer the sugar snap peas and scallions to the serving platter, leaving the oil in the pan.

Add the butter and let it melt. When it starts to foam, place the scallops in the pan in a single layer. Cook, without stirring, until the bottoms are golden brown, 2 to 3 minutes. Flip the scallops, sprinkle with the furikake, and pour in the yuzu juice. Cook until the scallops are just barely cooked through, 1 to 2 minutes. Transfer the scallops to the platter with the beans and pour the pan sauce over everything. Smear a little of the yuzu kosho on each scallop. Scatter the pea shoots over the top and serve.

/

Green beans and sugar snap peas electrify with an almost neon color when cooked until just tender. For the most vibrant color, be sure not to cook them for too long. Paint the scallops green with yuzu kosho, a Japanese condiment made from fermented green chiles, salt, and yuzu.

CILANTRO SCALLION PANCAKES

Makes eight 8-inch (20 cm) pancakes

1 bunch cilantro
1 tablespoon toasted sesame
     oil, plus more for brushing
Fine sea salt
3 cups (375 g) all-purpose
     flour, plus more for dusting
¾ cup (180 ml) boiling water
8 scallions, thinly sliced
Vegetable oil, for cooking

Rinse the cilantro and, while it's still dripping wet, put it in a food processor, stems and all. Add the sesame oil and a pinch of salt and purée.

Transfer the cilantro purée to a large bowl and add the flour. Pour in the boiling water and stir with a wooden spoon until a soft dough forms. Turn out the dough onto a floured work surface and knead until it's smooth and elastic, about 5 minutes. Cover with a clean kitchen towel and let rest for 30 minutes.

Divide the dough into 8 equal pieces. Using a floured rolling pin, roll each piece into a round about 8 inches (20 cm) in diameter. Brush with a thin layer of sesame oil, scatter about 1 tablespoon of the scallions on top, and sprinkle with a big pinch of salt. Roll up the dough to form a rope, then coil the rope around itself. Flatten the coil to an 8-inch (20 cm) round about ⅛ inch (3 mm) thick.

In a large skillet, heat 1 tablespoon vegetable oil over medium-high heat. Cook the pancakes one at a time until golden and crisp on the first side, 2 to 3 minutes. Flip and cook on the other side until golden and crisp, 2 to 3 minutes more. Serve hot.

/

Earthy forest green, with hints of golden brown, these savory pancakes taste best eaten hot and crisp straight from the skillet.

PEAR-APPLE CRUMBLE

Serves 6

½ cup (1 stick/115 g) unsalted butter, chilled and thinly sliced, plus more at room temperature for the baking dish

2 ripe pears, peeled, cored, and chopped into ¾-inch (2 cm) wedges

2 apples, peeled, cored, and chopped into ¾-inch (2 cm) wedges

¼ cup (50 g) granulated sugar

Finely grated zest of 1 lemon

1 tablespoon fresh lemon juice

1 cup (125 g) all-purpose flour

½ cup packed (105 g) brown sugar

½ cup (65 g) hazelnuts, toasted and chopped

⅓ cup (30 g) rolled oats

½ teaspoon fine sea salt

¼ teaspoon ground cinnamon

¼ teaspoon ground cardamom

2 teaspoons pure vanilla extract

Hazelnut gelato, for serving

Preheat the oven to 375°F (190°C). Butter a 9-inch (23 cm) square baking dish.

Combine the pears, apples, granulated sugar, lemon zest, and lemon juice in the prepared baking dish. Toss gently.

In a medium bowl, stir together the flour, brown sugar, hazelnuts, oats, salt, cinnamon, and cardamom. Using your fingertips, rub the butter into the flour mixture until there are no butter pieces larger than a pea. Add the vanilla and squeeze the mixture several times to form clumps. Scatter the streusel topping evenly over the pears and apples.

Bake until the topping is golden brown and the fruit is soft underneath, about 40 minutes. Serve warm, with a scoop of hazelnut gelato.

/

Teddy-bear brown. Topped with a big scoop of hazelnut gelato, this crumble is almost as comforting as a beloved stuffed animal.

PARSNIP SOUP WITH TOASTED SUNFLOWER SEEDS AND DATES

Serves 6

2 tablespoons unsalted butter
3 tablespoons extra-virgin
   olive oil
6 medium parsnips (about
   3 pounds/1.4 kg), peeled
   and cut into 1-inch (2.5 cm)
   pieces
1 small yellow onion, chopped
2 garlic cloves, sliced
Leaves from 3 sprigs thyme
Fine sea salt
4 cups (960 ml) good-quality
   chicken or vegetable broth
¼ cup (35 g) hulled sunflower
   seeds
Crème fraîche, for serving
6 dates, pitted and chopped

Heat a large pot over medium heat. Add the butter and 2 tablespoons of the olive oil. When the butter foams, add the parsnips, onion, garlic, thyme, and 1½ teaspoons salt. Cook, stirring often, until the onion softens, about 3 minutes. Pour in the broth and adjust the heat so the soup simmers, then cook until the parsnips are tender, 12 to 15 minutes.

Using an immersion blender, purée the soup directly in the pot until very smooth. (Alternatively, carefully transfer the soup to a countertop blender and blend until smooth.) Taste and season with more salt.

In a small skillet, combine the sunflower seeds and remaining 1 tablespoon olive oil and heat over medium heat, stirring often, until the sunflower seeds are golden, 3 minutes.

To serve, ladle the soup into bowls, swirl in a spoonful of crème fraîche, and sprinkle with the toasted sunflower seeds and dates.

/

A bowl to soothe. Tonal shades of beige and dirty blond, with accenting color from toasted sunflower seeds and slivers of date for sweetness.

CHIPOTLE-CUMIN PINTO AND CHORIZO ENFRIJOLADAS

Serves 4 to 6

2 cups (400 g) dried pinto
   beans
1 yellow onion
2 tablespoons extra-virgin
   olive oil
1 dried chipotle chile, stemmed
Fine sea salt
1 teaspoon ground cumin
½ teaspoon dried Mexican
   oregano
4 tablespoons (60 ml)
   vegetable oil
12 (6-inch/15 cm) corn
   tortillas
12 ounces (340 g) fresh
   (Mexican) chorizo

Place the beans in a large heavy-bottomed pot. Add enough water to cover the beans by about 2 inches (5 cm). Cut the onion in half, peel away the papery skin, and drop the two halves into the pot. Add the olive oil and chipotle. Bring the water to a lively boil and cook for 10 minutes, then lower the heat so the liquid barely simmers. Partially cover the pot and cook until the beans are completely soft all the way through, 1½ to 2 hours total, depending on the age of the beans. Every so often, uncover the pot, give the beans a stir, and check the water level. If the beans are poking out, add more hot water to submerge them. When the beans are almost done, stir in 1 teaspoon salt, wait a few minutes, then taste a bean and a sip of broth. Add more salt to taste, knowing that only the broth will taste salty at first and then the beans will slowly absorb the salt. Fish out and discard the onion halves but leave the chile. Stir in the cumin and oregano.

Transfer the beans and 1½ cups (360 ml) of their broth to a blender. Blend until smooth and the consistency of yogurt. Empty the pot, discarding any remaining broth, then return the bean sauce to the pot and bring to a boil. Lower the heat to low and keep the bean sauce warm.

Heat a large skillet over medium-high heat. Swirl in 2 tablespoons of the vegetable oil, then add 1 to 2 tortillas and fry until golden and starting to crisp, about 1 minute per side. Transfer to a plate and repeat with the remaining tortillas. Add the remaining 2 tablespoons oil and the chorizo to the pan and cook until browned, 7 to 9 minutes.

Use tongs to dip one fried tortilla in the bean sauce and set it on a serving plate. Spoon about 1 tablespoon of the chorizo in the center of the tortilla, then fold over the tortilla. Repeat with the remaining tortillas and chorizo. Sprinkle the last of the chorizo over the top and serve.

/

Like enchiladas except with beans (*frijoles* in Spanish). These are stuffed with fresh chorizo, but you could easily make a vegan version using soy-rizo.

BROWN BUTTER GNOCCHI WITH WILD MUSHROOMS AND BREAD CRUMBS

Serves 2

6 tablespoons (¾ stick/85 g)
    unsalted butter
½ cup (40 g) coarse fresh
    bread crumbs
1 garlic clove, minced
Fine sea salt
9 ounces (255 g) wild
    mushrooms, wiped clean
    and cut into bite-size pieces
    if large
Freshly ground black pepper
1 (14-ounce/400 g) package
    potato gnocchi

In a small saucepan, cook the butter over medium heat until it turns a deep grizzly-bear brown and smells nutty, 4 to 5 minutes.

Transfer half the browned butter to a large skillet. Add the bread crumbs, garlic, and ¼ teaspoon salt and cook over medium heat, stirring occasionally, until the bread crumbs are toasted and crunchy, 3 to 5 minutes. Transfer to a bowl and set aside.

Place the same skillet over medium-high heat. Add the remaining browned butter, then add the mushrooms and spread them into a single layer. Cook, without stirring, until the mushrooms are browned on the first side, 3 minutes. Sprinkle with ¼ teaspoon salt and several grinds of pepper. Stir and cook until well browned all over, 5 to 7 minutes more.

Bring a pot of generously salted water to a boil. Add the gnocchi and cook until they float to the surface. Using a slotted spoon, transfer the gnocchi directly to the pan with the mushrooms. Stir well and serve, with toasted bread crumbs scattered over the top.

/

Warm, golden-brown gnocchi tossed with buttery wild mushrooms and crunchy toasted bread crumbs.

PIRI-PIRI CHICKEN AND POTATOES

Serves 4

4 fresh red Fresno chiles,
    stemmed and coarsely
    chopped
4 dried chiles de árbol,
    stemmed and broken into
    pieces
1 shallot, coarsely chopped
4 garlic cloves, peeled
1 (2-inch/5 cm) piece fresh
    ginger, peeled and coarsely
    chopped
1½ teaspoons fine sea salt
1 teaspoon paprika
1 teaspoon dried oregano
Finely grated zest and juice of
    1 lemon
1 tablespoon sherry vinegar
½ cup (120 ml) extra-virgin
    olive oil
3½ pounds (1.6 kg) bone-in,
    skin-on chicken pieces
1½ pounds (680 g) Yukon Gold
    potatoes, cut into ¾-inch-
    thick (2 cm) wedges

In a food processor, combine the Fresno chiles, chiles de árbol, shallot, garlic, ginger, salt, paprika, oregano, lemon zest, lemon juice, vinegar, and olive oil. Process until smooth. Set aside about ½ cup (120 ml) of the pepper sauce. Pour the remaining sauce into a large bowl, add the chicken, cover, and let marinate at room temperature for 30 minutes or in the refrigerator for up to 3 days.

Preheat the oven to 450°F (230°C).

Use tongs to transfer the chicken to a rimmed baking sheet. Roast for 20 minutes.

Place the potato wedges on another rimmed baking sheet. Toss them with the reserved ½ cup (120 ml) pepper sauce. Roast the potatoes in the oven with the chicken until they are tender when poked with a fork and the chicken is cooked through, 20 to 25 minutes for the potatoes and about 45 minutes total for the chicken. Serve hot and crispy.

/

Ochre, the color of roasted chicken. Chiles (both fresh and dried) impart a little redness to the marinade here, but then a scorching-hot oven browns everything and the red fades to background warmth.

CARAMELIZED ONION AND ANCHOVY TART

Serves 4

1 sheet frozen puff pastry
3 tablespoons unsalted butter
3 large yellow onions, thinly
    sliced
Fine sea salt
1 tablespoon sherry vinegar
8 anchovies
1 large egg
1 tablespoon heavy cream

Preheat the oven to 425°F (220°C). Line a baking sheet with parchment paper.

Remove the puff pastry from the freezer and let it defrost at room temperature while you caramelize the onions.

In a large sauté pan, melt the butter over medium heat. Add a few handfuls of the sliced onion to the pan and cook, stirring occasionally, until they soften and make room for more onions, about 2 minutes. Continue adding handfuls of onion and cooking them until you've added them all. Stir in a couple of pinches of salt. Lower the heat to medium-low and cook, stirring every few minutes, until the onions are golden brown, 15 to 20 minutes. Cook, stirring more frequently as the onions brown further, until they are deeply caramelized, another 15 to 20 minutes. If the onions stick to the pan, add a splash of water and scrape the pan with a wooden spoon. Remove the pan from the heat, mix in the vinegar, and let the caramelized onions cool for a few minutes.

Unfold the puff pastry and place it on the prepared baking sheet. Use the tip of a small knife to score a border 1 inch (2.5 cm) in from the edge of the puff pastry. Spread the caramelized onions evenly over the pastry, staying within the border. Drape the anchovies on top of the onions.

Beat the egg with the cream to make an egg wash. Brush the egg wash over the exposed pastry border. Bake the tart until the crust is puffed and deep golden brown, 15 to 25 minutes. Serve hot or at room temperature.

/

Burnished to golden glory.

SLOW-ROASTED GUAJILLO PORK

Serves 8 to 12

5 dried guajillo chiles
Boiling water, as needed
4 garlic cloves, peeled
¼ cup (60 ml) extra-virgin
    olive oil
¼ cup (50 g) sugar
¼ cup (70 g) fine sea salt
1 (7- to 9-pound/3.2 to 4 kg)
    whole bone-in, skin-on
    pork shoulder

Break the guajillos into small pieces, keeping all the seeds but discarding the stems. Using a spice grinder or high-speed blender, grind them to a coarse powder. Transfer to a small bowl and stir in a splash of boiling water to rehydrate the chiles. Let them absorb it, then stir in a little more water, continuing to stir in splashes and adding as much as they'll take. Using a mortar and pestle, pound the garlic to a paste and stir it into the chiles. Mix in the olive oil.

In another small bowl, stir together the sugar and salt.

Place the pork skin-side up in a roasting pan large enough for it to fit snugly. Rub the sugar-salt mixture over the pork on all sides, then rub with the guajillo mixture. Cover with plastic wrap and refrigerate overnight or up to 3 days.

About 15 minutes before you're ready to cook the pork, preheat the oven to 300°F (150°C).

Remove the plastic and roast the pork until it's extremely tender when poked with a fork, 6 to 7 hours. Spoon out most of the rendered fat and reserve it in a small bowl. Shred the meat using two forks, mixing a little of the fat back in, if you like. Serve hot or warm.

/

A long and slow roast turns this pork grizzly-bear brown. The skin becomes crackly and charred.

MOCHA CAKE WITH GANACHE FROSTING

Serves 8

Unsalted butter, for the pan
1¼ cups (155 g) all-purpose
  flour
1 teaspoon baking powder
½ teaspoon baking soda
¾ teaspoon fine sea salt
¼ cup (20 g) unsweetened
  cocoa powder
1 tablespoon instant coffee
1 cup (240 ml) freshly brewed
  espresso or strong coffee
  (decaf, if you prefer)
1 cup packed (215 g) brown
  sugar
½ cup (120 g) plain whole-milk
  Greek yogurt
2 large eggs
½ cup (120 ml) neutral-
  flavored oil, such as canola
  or safflower
7 ounces (200 g) bittersweet
  chocolate, broken into
  small pieces
1 cup (240 ml) heavy cream

Preheat the oven to 350°F (175°C). Generously butter an 8-inch (20 cm) round cake pan and line the bottom with parchment paper cut to fit.

In a medium bowl, whisk together the flour, baking powder, baking soda, and salt.

In a large bowl, whisk together the cocoa powder, instant coffee, and ¾ cup (180 ml) of the espresso. Add the brown sugar, yogurt, and eggs. Whisk vigorously until smooth. Add the flour mixture and whisk until there are no visible streaks of flour. Whisk in the oil. Pour the batter into the prepared pan. Bake until the center of the cake springs back when lightly pressed, about 35 minutes.

Meanwhile, place the chocolate in a medium bowl. In a small saucepan, warm the cream over medium heat until bubbles appear around the edges of the pot. Stir in the remaining ¼ cup (60 ml) espresso, then pour the coffee-cream mixture over the chocolate. Let stand for 1 minute, then whisk until smooth. Set aside at room temperature until thickened.

Let the cake cool in the pan for 5 minutes before inverting it onto a wire rack, turning it right-side up, and letting it cool completely. Frost with the mocha ganache.

/

Chocolate and coffee—what a duo! Their flavors complement each other so beautifully, with the bitter edge of coffee softened by the sweetness of chocolate. And their colors match as well.

ESPRESSO GRANITA

Serves 6

2 cups (480 ml) freshly brewed
    espresso or strong coffee
    (decaf, if you prefer)
½ cup packed (105 g) brown
    sugar
1 tablespoon coffee liqueur

In a small bowl, combine the hot espresso and brown sugar and stir until the sugar dissolves completely. Stir in the liqueur. Pour the mixture into an 8-inch (20 cm) square baking dish or equivalent-size dish, cover tightly with a lid or plastic wrap, and freeze for at least 4 hours. At least once every hour, use a fork to lightly scrape the surface to break up the frozen coffee into tiny crystals. (If you forget to scrape the granita and it freezes solid, don't worry—it will still work. Just let it thaw very slightly, then use a fork to scrape and break it up into tiny crystals.) Once the granita has been scraped to a fluffy consistency, cover the dish again and freeze until ready to serve, up to 3 days.

Serve the granita in small chilled bowls.

/

A splash of coffee liqueur helps to keep this granita from freezing into a solid ice block. You can omit it, but if you do, be diligent about scraping the granita at regular intervals. Or, another brown alcohol, like whiskey, can be used instead.

GINGERY PORK UDON WITH FRIZZLED SHALLOTS

Serves 2 to 4

1 large or 2 small shallots, very thinly sliced

½ cup (120 ml) vegetable oil

2 tablespoons finely grated fresh ginger

4 garlic cloves, finely grated

½ yellow onion, finely chopped

8 ounces (225 g) ground pork

1 tablespoon white sesame paste

2 teaspoons rice vinegar

2 tablespoons soy sauce or tamari

1 tablespoon chile oil

1 pound (450 g) fresh or frozen udon noodles

White sesame seeds, toasted, for sprinkling

Line a plate with paper towels or a clean brown paper bag and set aside.

Place the shallots in a small saucepan and pour in the vegetable oil. Cook over medium-low heat, stirring occasionally, until the shallots are mostly brown (the thinnest slices will be the darkest), 10 to 18 minutes. Keep a close eye on the shallots once they are golden—they can go from brown to burnt pretty quickly! Strain the fried shallots through a fine-mesh sieve set over a bowl and then spread them out on the prepared plate.

Warm 3 tablespoons of the shallot oil in a stainless-steel skillet over medium-high heat. (Save the rest of the shallot oil for another recipe.) Add the ginger and garlic and cook, stirring continuously with a wooden spoon, until they smell delicious, about 1 minute. Stir in the onion and cook until it's tender, 3 to 4 minutes. Add the pork and cook, stirring and using the wooden spoon to break it up into small crumbly bits, until browned. Remove the pan from the heat and mix in the sesame paste, vinegar, soy sauce, and chile oil.

Bring a large pot of salted water to a boil. Add the udon noodles and cook according to the package instructions until al dente. Drain the noodles and transfer to serving bowls. Top each bowl with spoonfuls of the gingery pork, some frizzled shallots, and a sprinkle of sesame seeds.

/

Garlicky-ginger ground pork gains some flavor and smoothness from a spoonful of white sesame paste here. (In a pinch, you can use tahini.) But the real star of this dish might be the shower of thinly sliced shallots that are fried to a crisp.

CHILE NEGRO PORK TACOS WITH 50/50 TORTILLAS

Serves 4 to 6 (makes twelve 4-inch/10 cm tortillas)

Chile Negro Pork
2 pounds (910 g) boneless pork shoulder
Fine sea salt and freshly ground black pepper
2 ounces (57 g) dried chile negro peppers, stemmed
1 small yellow onion, peeled and quartered
4 tomatillos, husks removed and halved
3 garlic cloves, peeled
1½ teaspoons cumin seeds
½ cup (120 ml) boiling water
2 tablespoons vegetable oil

Tortillas
1 cup (115 g) blue corn masa harina
1 cup (125 g) all-purpose flour
1 tablespoon unsweetened noir (extra-dark) cocoa powder
1 teaspoon baking powder
1 teaspoon fine sea salt
5 tablespoons (65 g) lard
1 cup (240 ml) hot water
Vegetable oil, for the pan

/

Chile negro peppers are such a dark shade of brown that they appear to be black. These tortillas are made with blue masa harina and tinted with just a little bit of cocoa noir so that they become black, too.

Make the pork: Cut the pork into 6 pieces and sprinkle with ½ teaspoon salt and lots of black pepper. Place it in a container, cover, and refrigerate for at least 1 hour or up to 3 days.

Preheat the oven to 325°F (165°C).

In a Dutch oven or other oven-safe pot, toast the chiles over medium-high heat, flipping them with tongs, until fragrant and flexible, 2 to 4 minutes total. Transfer them to a plate. Put the onion and tomatillos in the pan, cut-side down, and cook, without stirring, until charred in a few places, about 5 minutes. Transfer to the plate with the chiles. Remove the pan from the heat, add the garlic and cumin, stir them around, and let them toast in the residual heat.

Transfer the toasted chiles to a blender and grind to a coarse powder. Pour in half the boiling water and blend to combine. Pour in the remaining water and blend again. Add the charred tomatillos, onion, garlic, cumin, and ¼ teaspoon salt. Blend until smooth.

Return the Dutch oven to medium-high heat. Use paper towels to pat the pork completely dry. Swirl in the vegetable oil, then add half the pork in a single layer and cook, without stirring, until browned on the first side, about 4 minutes. Flip and cook on the other side until browned, 2 to 4 minutes more. Use tongs to move the browned pork to a plate and repeat to sear the remaining pork. Return all the meat to the pot and pour in the chile sauce. Cover and transfer the pot to the oven. Bake until the meat is falling-apart tender, about 3 hours.

Meanwhile, make the tortillas: In a medium bowl, stir together the masa harina, flour, cocoa noir, baking powder, and salt. Use your fingertips to rub the lard into the flour mixture. Stir in the hot water, then knead the dough for 3 to 5 minutes. Divide the dough into 12 equal-size balls. Cover with a clean kitchen towel and let rest at room temperature for 30 minutes.

Using a tortilla press or a rolling pin, flatten each ball to a 4- to 5-inch (10 to 12.5 cm) circle. Heat a lightly oiled cast-iron skillet over medium heat for 2 minutes. Working with one dough round at a time, place it in the skillet and cook until puffed and golden brown in a few places on the first side, about 1 minute. Flip and cook on the second side for another 1 minute. Wrap the cooked tortilla in a clean kitchen towel to keep it soft while you cook the remaining dough.

When the pork is done, shred it, and spoon onto a warm tortilla.

KURO GOMA BUCKWHEAT WAFFLES

Serves 4 to 6

½ cup (120 ml) warm water
1 (¼-ounce/7 g) packet active
    dry yeast (2¼ teaspoons)
1 cup (200 g) sugar
2 cups (480 ml) sweetened oat
    milk, slightly warmed
½ cup (120 ml) vegetable oil,
    plus more for the waffle iron
1¾ cups (220 g) all-purpose
    flour
¼ cup (40 g) buckwheat flour
2 tablespoons unsweetened
    noir (extra-dark) cocoa
    powder
2 tablespoons kuro goma
    (black sesame) latte
    powder
½ teaspoon fine sea salt
2 large eggs
½ teaspoon baking soda
Pure maple syrup, for serving

Pour the warm water into a large bowl. Sprinkle the yeast and 2 tablespoons of the sugar evenly over the top and stir to dissolve. Cover the bowl with a clean kitchen towel and set aside until foamy, about 5 minutes.

Whisk in the remaining ¾ cup plus 2 tablespoons (175 g) sugar, the warm oat milk, vegetable oil, all-purpose flour, buckwheat flour, cocoa noir, latte powder, and salt. Cover the batter and let stand at room temperature for 1 hour or refrigerate for up to 3 days.

When you're ready to cook the waffles, preheat a waffle iron.

Whisk the eggs and baking soda into the batter.

Grease the waffle iron with oil (even if it's nonstick), spoon about 1 cup (240 ml) of the batter onto the waffle iron, close the lid, and cook according to the manufacturer's instructions until crisp. Transfer the waffle to a plate and repeat with the remaining batter. Serve warm, drizzled with maple syrup.

/

These waffles may appear to be burnt to a crisp, but they are actually perfectly cooked. You can drizzle them with maple syrup, which is dark brown enough that the deep color of the dish will be preserved.

TINY COCOA NOIR POTS DE CRÈME

Serves 8 to 10

2 large egg yolks
1 cup (240 ml) heavy cream
⅓ cup (30 g) unsweetened noir
   (extra-dark) cocoa powder,
   plus more for dusting
2 tablespoons cornstarch
½ cup (100 g) sugar
¼ teaspoon ground cardamom
¼ teaspoon fine sea salt
2 cups (480 ml) whole milk
2 teaspoons pure vanilla
   extract
3 ounces (85 g) dark
   chocolate, chopped

In a small bowl, stir together the egg yolks and ½ cup (120 ml) of the cream.

In a large heavy-bottomed pot, combine the cocoa noir, cornstarch, sugar, cardamom, and salt. Slowly whisk in the milk. Set the pot over medium heat and cook, whisking often to dissolve the sugar, until the mixture bubbles. Remove the pot from the heat. Whisk a ladleful of the cocoa mixture into the yolk-cream mixture, then slowly whisk the warmed yolk-cream mixture back into the pot. Set the pot over medium-low heat and cook, whisking often, just until it bubbles again, 2 to 3 minutes.

Add the vanilla and chocolate to the pot and whisk until the chocolate has melted. Pour the pudding into any kind of tiny cups you have, such as espresso cups or little ramekins. Press a piece of plastic wrap directly against the surface of each pudding, if you don't want a pudding skin to form, and refrigerate the puddings for at least 3 hours.

Just before serving, whip the remaining ½ cup (120 ml) cream. (You can sweeten it with confectioners' sugar, if you like, though I usually prefer to leave it as is.) Spoon a little whipped cream on top of each pudding and dust with cocoa noir.

/

These petite chocolate puddings are intensely chocolatey. They need the counterbalance of light whipped cream, but to keep the color theme you can obscure the cream by dusting it with cocoa noir powder.

PEPPERCORN-CRUSTED STEAK WITH BLACK GARLIC PAN SAUCE

Serves 4

5 tablespoons (70 g) unsalted butter
2 tablespoons coarsely cracked black peppercorns
2 tablespoons brown sugar
2 teaspoons fine sea salt
1 pound (450 g) skirt steak, cut in half to fit the pan
2 tablespoons vegetable oil
3 cloves black garlic, thinly sliced
¼ cup (60 ml) red wine
¾ cup (180 ml) good-quality chicken broth or beef broth

In a small microwave-safe bowl, combine 3 tablespoons of the butter, the peppercorns, brown sugar, and salt. Microwave until the butter melts, then stir to dissolve the sugar. Rub the mixture all over the steak and let the steak warm up at room temperature for 30 minutes to 1 hour.

Heat a large, nonreactive heavy-bottomed pan over high heat for 2 minutes. Swirl in 1 tablespoon of the vegetable oil, then add one half of the steak. Cook, turning after 2 minutes, until medium-rare on the inside (130°F/54°C if you're using an instant-read thermometer) and charred on the outside, about 4 minutes total. Transfer the steak to a carving board and let rest for 10 minutes. Repeat with the remaining steak (no need to add more oil).

While the steak rests, discard everything in the pan except the bits that are stuck to the bottom. Return the still-hot pan to the stovetop, off the heat. Add the remaining 1 tablespoon oil and the black garlic and let the garlic sizzle in the pan. Pour in the wine, set the heat to medium, and use a wooden spoon to scrape up the flavorful bits stuck to the bottom of the pan. When the wine has reduced in volume by about half, pour in the broth. Bring to a simmer and cook until slightly reduced, 5 minutes. Add the remaining 2 tablespoons butter and stir until melted and incorporated.

Slice the steak and serve with the black garlic sauce.

/

Tons of coarsely cracked black pepper creates a dark crust for this steak, and the pan sauce gets its shade from black garlic, which is regular garlic that has been gently cooked for weeks until the cloves turn black.

FORBIDDEN RICE TEMAKI

Serves 6

2 cups (400 g) uncooked
    black rice (Forbidden Rice)
3 cups (720 ml) water
6 tablespoons (90 ml) rice
    vinegar
3 tablespoons sugar
½ teaspoon fine sea salt
12 ounces (340 g) sashimi-
    grade boneless, skinless
    ahi tuna fillet
1 tablespoon toasted
    sesame oil
3 tablespoons soy sauce or
    tamari
8 sheets nori, cut in half
Black sesame seeds,
    for sprinkling

In a medium saucepan, combine the rice and water. Bring to a simmer, then cover and cook over low heat until the rice is tender and has absorbed all the water, about 30 minutes. Remove from the heat, keep covered with the lid, and let rest for 10 minutes.

In a small bowl, stir together the vinegar, sugar, and salt until the sugar dissolves completely.

When the rice is done, transfer it to a wide, shallow bowl and sprinkle the seasoned vinegar over it. Use a rice paddle or flat spatula to gently toss the rice to cool it down.

Using a very sharp knife, cut the tuna into ½-inch (1.5 cm) cubes. Place them in a shallow dish, pour in the sesame oil and soy sauce, and mix gently.

Dry your hands thoroughly and place a piece of nori, shiny-side down, in the palm of your nondominant hand. Spread ¼ to ½ cup (50 to 100 g) of the rice in an even layer across the left half of the nori. Sprinkle with sesame seeds. Arrange a heaping spoonful of the soy-sauced tuna diagonally across the rice. Cup your palm to bring the bottom-left corner in toward the center of the nori. Tuck it in and roll the nori around the rice into a cone shape. To help the nori stick to itself, put a grain of rice under the end of the nori and gently press to seal. Serve right away.

/

Crinkly, shiny nori wrapped around black Forbidden Rice makes both ingredients look even blacker. The ahi tuna soaks in a flavorful bath of dark soy sauce and becomes tinted as well.

SQUID INK PASTA WITH OIL-CURED OLIVES AND OPAL BASIL

Serves 4 to 6

3 cups (375 g) all-purpose flour
3 large eggs
3 large egg yolks
2 tablespoons extra-virgin olive oil
1 tablespoon squid ink
Semolina, for dusting
½ cup (90 g) oil-cured olives, pitted
3 tablespoons unsalted butter
1 cup (20 g) fresh opal basil, small leaves left whole and large leaves sliced into thin ribbons
Freshly ground black pepper

Measure the flour into a large bowl and make a well in the center, like a volcano. Add the eggs, egg yolks, olive oil, and squid ink to the well. Use a fork to stir, gently scraping in flour from the sides a little at a time. When the dough becomes too stiff to stir, use your hands to mix it, then turn it out onto a clean work surface and knead it into a ball. Cover and let rest at room temperature for 30 minutes.

Use your hands to flatten the dough ball into a disc, then cut it into 12 equal pieces. Work with one piece at a time and keep the other pieces covered with a clean kitchen towel. Flatten each piece with a rolling pin before passing it through a pasta machine set to the widest setting. Fold the dough lengthwise over itself into thirds, as if you were folding a letter, then pass it through on the widest setting again. Repeat once more to further knead the dough, then decrease the width setting of the machine by one notch and crank the dough through the rollers. Continue decreasing the width setting and passing the dough through until the sheet is long and just under $\frac{1}{16}$ inch (1.5 mm) thick (the second-thinnest setting on most machines).

Attach the noodle-cutting attachment to the pasta machine. Cut each sheet into noodles, generously dust with semolina to prevent sticking, and curl them into little nests. Place the noodle nests on a piece of parchment paper, cover, and refrigerate until ready to cook.

To cook, bring a large pot of generously salted water to a boil. Add the noodles, stir, and cook until al dente, about 5 minutes. Scoop up and reserve 1 cup (240 ml) of the cooking water before draining the pasta.

In a large skillet, warm the olives and butter over medium-high heat. Add the drained pasta directly to the pan along with half the reserved cooking water. Cook, stirring continuously, until the sauce emulsifies and coats the noodles, 1 to 2 minutes. (There should be a little liquid pooling in the skillet. If not, add more pasta water until you've got a light sauce.) Serve right away, sprinkled with the basil and topped with freshly ground black pepper.

/

Squid ink–tinted noodles and wrinkly oil-cured olives plus opal basil come together for this shadowy pasta dish.

CHIA PUDDINGS
WITH BLACKBERRIES

Serves 2 or 3

2 cups (480 ml) sweetened
  oat milk
½ cup (80 g) black chia seeds
¼ teaspoon pure vanilla
  extract
⅓ cup (105 g) blackberry jam
1 cup (145 g) fresh blackberries

In a medium bowl, whisk together the oat milk, chia seeds, and vanilla. Stir continuously for 20 to 30 seconds to disperse the chia seeds and break up any clumps. Let the mixture stand for about 5 minutes, then stir continuously for another 20 to 30 seconds. Pour the mixture into two or three serving bowls, cover, and refrigerate until thickened, at least 2 hours.

To serve, swirl some blackberry jam into each bowl of pudding and top with the blackberries.

/

Tiny specks of black chia seeds among the white oat milk create a dot effect here, tricking the eye into seeing a gray halftone color.

BLACK SESAME GELATO AND BRITTLE

Makes about 1 quart (1 L)
gelato and 1 large sheet
of brittle

Gelato
2 cups (480 ml) whole milk
1 cup (240 ml) heavy cream
⅔ cup packed (140 g) brown
  sugar
¼ teaspoon fine sea salt
6 large egg yolks
⅔ cup (190 g) Japanese-style
  black sesame paste

Brittle
Melted butter, for brushing
¼ cup packed (55 g) brown
  sugar
¼ cup (85 g) honey
¼ teaspoon fine sea salt
1 cup (140 g) black sesame
  seeds

/

Black sesame paste, lightened
by milk and cream, is
partnered here with midnight-
black sesame seed brittle.

Make the gelato: In a medium saucepan, combine the milk, cream, brown sugar, and salt. Warm over medium heat, whisking occasionally, until the sugar dissolves and the mixture is barely simmering.

In a medium bowl, whisk the egg yolks to break them up. While whisking continuously, slowly stream in about ¼ cup (60 ml) of the hot cream mixture and whisk to incorporate. Pour the tempered egg yolk mixture into the pot with the remaining hot cream and cook over medium-low heat, stirring continuously with a wooden spoon or rubber spatula, until the custard thickens enough to coat the back of the spoon and registers 155°F (68°C) on an instant-read thermometer, about 5 minutes. Strain the custard through a fine-mesh sieve into a large bowl. Add the black sesame paste and use an immersion blender to incorporate it into the custard. Cover with a piece of plastic wrap pressed directly against the surface of the custard and refrigerate for at least 4 hours and up to 2 days.

Meanwhile, make the brittle: Cut two large sheets of parchment paper and brush them with melted butter on one side. Have a rolling pin nearby.

In a small saucepan, combine the brown sugar, honey, and salt. Cook over medium heat, swirling the pan but not stirring at all, until the mixture darkens, foams, and smells deeply toasted, about 5 minutes. Remove the pan from the heat, add the black sesame seeds, and quickly stir them in with a rubber spatula. Immediately transfer the mixture to the buttered side of one of the prepared parchment sheets, cover with the other sheet, buttered-side down, and roll it out as thin as possible before the brittle hardens. Let cool completely.

Transfer the chilled custard to an ice cream maker and churn according to the manufacturer's instructions. You can serve it right from the ice cream maker or you can transfer the gelato to a freezer-safe container, press a piece of parchment paper directly against the surface of the gelato, cover tightly with the lid, and store in the back of the freezer until ready to serve. Before serving, let the gelato warm up for a few minutes at room temperature until scoopable. Break the brittle into pieces and serve it with the gelato.

MIDNIGHT CUPCAKES

Makes 12 cupcakes

Cupcakes
1 cup (125 g) all-purpose flour
1 cup (200 g) sugar
¼ cup (25 g) unsweetened
   natural cocoa powder
2 tablespoons unsweetened
   noir (extra-dark) cocoa
   powder
¾ teaspoon baking powder
¼ teaspoon baking soda
¼ teaspoon fine sea salt
6 tablespoons (¾ stick/85 g)
   unsalted butter, melted
   and cooled slightly
2 large eggs
2 teaspoons pure vanilla
   extract
⅓ cup (80 ml) freshly brewed
   espresso or strong coffee
   (decaf, if you prefer)
2 tablespoons vegetable oil

Cocoa Frosting
3½ ounces (100 g) dark
   chocolate, chopped
4 tablespoons (½ stick/57 g)
   unsalted butter, cut into
   4 pieces
2 tablespoons unsweetened
   noir (extra-dark) cocoa
   powder
Pinch of fine sea salt

Make the cupcakes: Preheat the oven to 350°F (175°C). Line a 12-well cupcake pan with paper liners.

In the bowl of a stand mixer fitted with the whisk attachment, combine the flour, sugar, both cocoa powders, the baking powder, baking soda, and salt. Mix on low speed to combine. Add the melted butter, eggs, and vanilla and mix on medium speed until fully incorporated, about 1 minute. Drizzle in the espresso and vegetable oil and mix on medium speed for 1 minute.

Divide the batter evenly among the prepared wells of the cupcake pan. Bake until springy when pressed lightly and a toothpick inserted into the center of a cupcake comes out without any wet batter clinging to it, about 20 minutes. Let cool.

Make the frosting: Place the chocolate in a heat-safe bowl set over a pot of simmering water and let it melt, without stirring more than once or twice. Add the butter, cocoa noir, and salt and stir gently to combine. When all the butter has melted, remove the bowl from the heat. Place in the refrigerator to cool, stirring every so often, until thick enough to spread, about 15 minutes.

Spread a generous dollop of frosting on top of each cooled cupcake.

/

These are the yin to the yang of Wedding Gown Cupcakes (page 32). Dark, dark chocolate that appears as black as licorice.

BLACK TAHINI COOKIES

Makes 12 cookies

¾ cup plus 2 tablespoons
(110 g) all-purpose flour
2 tablespoons buckwheat flour
½ teaspoon baking powder
¼ teaspoon baking soda
½ teaspoon fine sea salt
6 tablespoons (¾ stick/85 g)
unsalted butter, at room
temperature
¼ cup plus 2 tablespoons
packed (80 g) brown sugar
1 large egg
⅓ cup (95 g) black tahini
1 teaspoon pure vanilla extract
Scant ½ cup (70 g) black
sesame seeds

Preheat the oven to 350°F (175°C). Line a baking sheet with parchment paper.

In a medium bowl, whisk together the all-purpose flour, buckwheat flour, baking powder, baking soda, and salt.

In the bowl of a stand mixer fitted with the paddle attachment, beat the butter and brown sugar on medium-high speed until fluffy and lightened in color, about 4 minutes. Add the egg, beat for 1 minute, and then add the black tahini and vanilla. Beat until fully incorporated. Stir in the flour mixture until just combined.

Put the black sesame seeds in a wide, shallow dish or on a plate with a lip. Using two small spoons, scoop the (very sticky!) dough into 12 golf ball–size balls, roll them in the black sesame seeds, and place them evenly spaced apart on the prepared baking sheet. Bake until the cookies smell toasted and have spread out into half spheres, 12 to 14 minutes. It's tricky to see when these dark cookies are done; better to underdo it slightly than to overbake them. Let cool on the baking sheet. (They'll firm up a little as they cool.)

/

A thorough coating of black sesame seeds gives these cookies an even darker appearance and makes them look like they have the rough, pebbly texture of alligator skin.

COLOR MENUS

There are many reasons for putting together a color-focused menu. Maybe you're celebrating your team's championship win. Or maybe you're hosting a graduation party and want to highlight the school colors. You might want to choose recipes that are the same colors as the flag of a country you visited on vacation. Color menus are also beautiful ways to reinforce the palette chosen for a wedding, birthday party, or other celebration. Certain colors grouped together bring to mind specific holidays—red and green dishes on a Christmas dinner table, for example. Here are some sample menus to inspire festive gatherings of all kinds.

SPRING

Each season has a certain color palette and coordinating flavors that go with it. This spring menu brings together pastels and delicate flavors.

/

Apple-Fennel Salad with Goat Cheese and Pistachio Pesto

Turmeric-Pickled Egg Salad

Blueberry Branzino

Blue Jean Easter Egg Breads

Guava-Rhubarb Sorbet

FALL

Fall is everyone's favorite time of year, when the weather cools and a new school year starts. A fall harvest menu has the colors of changing leaves, October pumpkins, and the verdant flash of pine tree green.

/

Parsnip Soup with Toasted Sunflower Seeds and Dates

Persimmon-Kumquat Salad with Goji Dressing and Nasturtiums

French Lentils, Broccolini, and Arugula with Italian Salsa Verde

Brown Butter Gnocchi with Wild Mushrooms and Bread Crumbs

Pear-Apple Crumble

MONO-CHROME: ORANGE

A monochrome menu is a fun way to eat your favorite color. This one celebrates the bounty and beauty of orange—it's flashy, bright, and invigorating.

/

Sungold Tomato Gazpacho

Habanero Cara Cara Salmon Poke

Ribboned Carrots on Harissa Yogurt

Spicy Kabocha Tempura

Saffron-Tangerine Frozen Yogurt

MONO-CHROME: GREEN

Is there a color that feels fresher than green? Celebrate the natural beauty of this hue with an all-green menu or use it for a green-lover's birthday party, a St. Patrick's Day meal with some new flavors, or a graduation from a school with green colors—there are many opportunities for a monochrome menu.

/

Zhoug-Marinated Feta and Fava Toasts

Cilantro Scallion Pancakes

Blistered Beans and Yuzu Kosho Scallops

Matcha-Lime Teacake with Candied Mint

Matcha and Mint Ice Cream Sundae

RAINBOW

Ideal for celebrating Pride, this rainbow menu includes a recipe from every color section (except white and black).

/

Piri-Piri Chicken and Potatoes

Cherry Tomato Agrodolce with 'Nduja on Toast

Baked Macaroni and Squash

New Potato Salad with Creamy Mustard and Garlic Chips

Little Gem Caesar with Spinach Croutons

Butterfly Pea Flower Ice Cream

Uva Ube Schiacciata

Beet-Balls with Pickled Turnip Dip

BLACK AND WHITE

This combination of colors is classic and feels modern, chic, and fancy. An elegant menu for a dress-up affair.

Radish, Belgian Endive, and Ricotta Salata

Garlicky Gigante Beans, Salt-and-Vin Cauliflower, and Pine Nuts

Squid Ink Pasta with Oil-Cured Olives and Opal Basil

Peppercorn-Crusted Steak with Black Garlic Pan Sauce

Pavlova with Vanilla Cream, White Dragon Fruit, and Nectarines

VALENTINE

For lovers, galentines, besties, and soul mates. This menu is romantic and brings together all the rosy tones and flavors.

Pomelo Hamachi Crudo

Beets, Blood Oranges, and Radicchio

Slow-Roasted Harissa Salmon and Pink Chicory Salad

Wine-Poached Pears with Sour Cherry Cream and Roses

Rose-Glasses Fortune Cookies

RED, WHITE, AND BLUE

For a Fourth of July party, Labor Day BBQ, or even a French Bastille Day fête.

/

Tomato Tart

Coppa-Wrapped Jimmy Nardellos

Pita, Chamomile-Steeped Burrata, and Hawaiian Honey

Blueberry Branzino

Tzatziki Couscous

Chicken-Jicama Salad with Cumin Crema

Ombré Crêpe Cake

Marbled Sugar Cookies

HALLOWEEN

Any holiday or event that already has an established color scheme is an opportunity to cook color. These orange and black dishes for Halloween fit right in with the spooky theme.

/

Spicy Kabocha Tempura

Forbidden Rice Temaki

Sweet Potato Rösti with Gochujang Sour Cream

Black Sesame Gelato and Brittle

CHRISTMAS

If you're looking to start a new tradition for the holidays, try a color-themed menu. These red and green dishes taste festive and even a little glamorous.

/

Zhoug-Marinated Feta and Fava Toasts

Bavette with Romesco, Pluots, and Sherried Cherries

Kale Risotto

Red Berry Porridge with Sugar Plum Compote

TROPICAL

Consider creating a menu in which both the flavors and the colors evoke a mood . . . this one being that of a beachside vacation! The colors and flavors are breezy and light.

/

Spanish-Style Garlic Shrimp

Udon in Spicy Coconut Broth

Sky Dumplings

Blue Madeleines

JEWEL TONES

A collection of the most vibrantly hued recipes that look like precious gems. This menu would be perfect for Mardi Gras.

/

Pineapple Chicken Satay with Sunshine Sauce

Lemongrass-Cilantro Tofu Bánh Mì

Ahi Tuna Aguachile Rojo

Purple Sweet Potato Pie Bars with Cornmeal Crust

ACKNOWLEDGMENTS

When I began writing cookbooks, my name never appeared on the cover. I started in the quiet, inconspicuous roles like recipe tester or coauthor, and I worked my way up from there. During those early years, I formed a habit of reading the acknowledgments before any other page. I've never forgotten the sense of pride that rose in my chest when I saw my name. Now that I have the honor of writing these acknowledgments, I feel particularly attuned to the importance of crediting and thanking the many people whose contributions brought this cookbook to life.

I will forever be grateful to my dear friend and agent, Katherine Cowles, for coming up with the idea for this book. Kitty, you astonish me with your brilliance. Thank you for always believing in me and envisioning a future for my work. Much love to Carson Kraft for your friendship and inspiration, too!

Thank you very much to the entire team at Artisan, especially Lia Ronnen, Bella Lemos, and Judy Pray. You three smart, talented, and keenly intuitive women are collaborators whom I hope to have in my corner for the rest of my career. Many thanks to Karen Tongish, Sibylle Kazeroid, and Hillary Leary for managing editorial; and to Nancy Murray and Donna Brown for overseeing production. The stunning design of this book is all thanks to Vanessa Holden, with assistance from Jane Treuhaft and Suet Chong. Thank you to Theresa Collier, Amy Michelson, and Fiona Winch for publicity. I'm a somewhat shy writer who is most at ease hiding behind my desk or cooking at home and I wouldn't say my strongest skill set is promoting myself or my books, but you are all so good at your jobs that you somehow make it enjoyable and fun.

The photographs and food styling are the genius work of David Malosh and Simon Andrews, respectively. Thank you both for making my recipes look like they're having their best-ever hair days.

Copy editors are the guardian angels of books, and I am incredibly fortunate that Ivy McFadden's eyes were on every word in this book. Thanks for your careful, detailed work and your deep understanding of food culture.

Thank you to Aya Brackett for photographing my author portrait. I love the artful way you see the world, and I cherish our friendship.

I've been fortunate to learn from some of the best chefs. Suzanne Goin, you started it all! Thank you so much for taking a big chance on an enthusiastic grad student. What would I do without you? Thanks also to Liz Prueitt, Chad Robertson, Yotam Ottolenghi, Noor Murad, Nadiya Hussain, Nigel Slater, Yasmin Khan, Christina Tosi, Claire Saffitz, Deborah Madison, Roxana Jullapat, and Alice Waters.

A huge thank you to the booksellers and librarians who have recommended my cookbooks and put them in the hands of readers and eaters. My hometown independent bookstore, East Bay Booksellers, is a real gem, staffed by such generous and intelligent people.

To my family and friends, thank you for supporting me, cheering me on, and loving me unconditionally. Your hugs and late-night texts sustain me. Let's celebrate this book and share a meal together soon!

Sonia Guerrero, thank you from the bottom of my heart for caring for Arturito while I wrote this cookbook. Our family grew when we met you. Thanks for teaching me about the dark color of chile negro and how to use strawberries to sweeten agua de jamaica.

Last, and most important, thank you to Graham Willis Bradley. You are the love of my life, you give meaning to everything I do, and you make me a better person. Without you, this cookbook (and my other books) would not exist, and I'm not quite sure where I'd be either. Thank you so much for encouraging me to stretch outside of my recipe development comfort zone, to get weird, to try new ideas and nontraditional flavor combinations. Thank you for handing me a stack of color theory books at the start of this project and for continuously showing me the ways in which food and design are interwoven. I love you and Arthur more than I could ever explain. You two fill my world with joyous color.

SOURCES

INGREDIENTS

Amarena Cherries

Market Hall Foods
markethallfoods.com

Anchovies

Ortiz
conservasortiz.com

Patagonia Provisions
patagoniaprovisions.com

The Spanish Table
spanishtable.com

Wild Planet
wildplanetfoods.com

Beet Powder, Dragon Fruit Powder, Butterfly Pea Flower Powder, and Spirulina

Suncore Foods
suncorefoods.com

Cheese

Bellwether Farms
bellwetherfarms.com

Laura Chenel's Chèvre, Inc.
laurachenel.com

Murray's
murrayscheese.com

Point Reyes Farmstand Cheese Co.
pointreyescheese.com

Chocolate and Cocoa Powder

Guittard Chocolate Company
guittard.com

King Arthur Baking Company
kingarthurbaking.com

Valrhona
valrhona-chocolate.com

Dates

Rancho Meladuco
ranchomeladuco.com

Doubanjiang (Sichuan Chile Bean Paste)

Fly by Jing
flybyjing.com

Dried Beans, Grains, and Pasta

Anson Mills
ansonmills.com

Rancho Gordo
ranchogordo.com

Sfoglini
sfoglini.com

Dried Hibiscus and Blue Corn Masa Harina

Masienda
masienda.com

Gochugaru and Gochujang

Mother-in-Law's
milkimchi.com

Rhei-Maid
rheimaid.com

Harissa

New York Shuk
nyshuk.com

Honey and Bee Pollen

Bees Knees
bushwickkitchen.com

Bee Local
beelocal.com

Bee Raw
beeraw.com

Kiss the Flower
kisstheflower.com

Savannah Bee Company
savannahbee.com

Wedderspoon
wedderspoon.com

Zach & Zoë Sweet Bee Farm
zachandzoe.co

Kuro Goma (Black Sesame) Latte Powder

Kuki Sangyo
japanesetaste.com

'Nduja, Coppa, and Other Cured Meats

Fra' Mani Handcrafted Foods
framani.com

La Quercia
laquerciashop.com

Olympia Provisions
olympiaprovisions.com

Olive Oil

California Olive Ranch
californiaoliveranch.com

Enzo Olive Oil
enzooliveoil.com

Exau
exauoliveoil.com

Fat Gold
fat.gold

Pineapple Collaborative
pineapplecollaborative.com

Séka Hills
sekahills.com

Orange Blossom Water and Rose Water

Maalouf

Nielsen-Massey
nielsenmassey.com

Sahadi's
sahadis.com

Salt and Spices

Burlap & Barrel
burlapandbarrel.com

Diaspora Co.
diasporaco.com

Jacobsen Salt Co.
jacobsensalt.com

Kalustyan's
kalustyans.com

Maldon Salt Company
maldonsalt.co.uk

Moonflowers (for saffron)
moonflowers.co

Oaktown Spice Shop
oaktownspiceshop.com

Penzeys Spices
penzeys.com

Zingerman's
zingermans.com

Tahini and Sesame Paste

Belazu
belazu.com

Nouka Black Sesame Paste

Seed + Mill
seedandmill.com

Tofu

Hodo
hodofoods.com

Joodooboo
joodooboo.co

Wine

Kermit Lynch Wine Merchant
kermitlynch.com

Ordinaire
ordinairewine.com

HOME AND KITCHEN SUPPLIES

Anthropologie
anthropologie.com

Àplat
aplat.com

Brook Farm General Store
brookfarmgeneralstore.com

Crate & Barrel
crateandbarrel.com

Food52
food52.com

Heath Ceramics
heathceramics.com

Indigo
chapters.indigo.ca

Kaufmann Mercantile
kaufmann-mercantile.com

March
marchsf.com

Muji
muji.us

Schoolhouse
schoolhouse.com

Smeg
smeg.com

Sur La Table
surlatable.com

Williams Sonoma
williams-sonoma.com

INDEX

AYA BRACKETT

Maria Zizka is the author and coauthor of numerous award-winning cookbooks, including *The Newlywed Table*, *One-Bowl Meals*, and *Boards, Platters, Plates*. She studied biology at UC Berkeley and food culture at UNISG in northern Italy, where she now teaches as a visiting lecturer. She was named by *Forbes* as one of the most influential people under thirty in the world of food and drink. Zizka lives and cooks in the Berkeley Hills with her husband and son. Her favorite color to eat is green. Follow her on Instagram at @mariazizka.